C C S U

ENGLISH

The Connecticut Literary Anthology 2020

Executive Editor: Jotham Burrello

Submission Manager: Bailey Mackowitz
Genre Editors: Kristiana Torres, Kathryn Fitzpatrick,
Shayna Shattelroe
Guest Editors: Colin Holston, Lucy Ferriss, Ines Rivera
Readers: Janay Wynter, Marx Chiriboga, Andrew Jacobs, Ariella
Ozuna Mendoza, Claire Hibbs-Cusson, Conor Breen

The anthology was generously supported by an anonymous donor grant, which was administered by the Hartford Foundation for Public Giving.

www.ccsu.edu/english/whyenglish.html

ISBN: 978-1-7324141-4-3

Library of Congress Control Number: 2020946145

Printed in the United States of America

Book Design by Jillian Goeler, Jag Ink
Interior Design by Eswari Kamireddy

First Edition
10 9 8 7 6 5 4 3 2 1

CCSU English Department
New Britain, Connecticut

For All Connecticut Readers and Writers

CONTENTS

INTRODUCTION

Arts funding is a precious commodity, and funding for non-profit literary publishing is really scarce. So when I received an email in spring 2019 that an anonymous donor was interested in partnering with a college English department to publish an anthology of Connecticut writers, I thought I had won the lottery. Okay, it wasn't quite "quit your day job and publish from Tahiti" money, but rather a fine investment to celebrate Nutmeg authors, and an opportunity for Central Connecticut State University students to earn a little gas money as they learned how to edit, produce, and market a book.

Starting in fall 2019, our team of student editors and marketers began to build the infrastructure to publish the inaugural Connecticut Literary Anthology. When the virus hit in February, we were on our way to receiving three hundred submissions of poetry and prose. We read blind, meaning we did not know the author of each submission. Our submission guidelines had one key criteria: that writers reside in Connecticut on January 1, 2020. After a brief hiatus to relocate from campus to home offices in March, our readers and editors whittled the three hundred submissions down to a few dozen and then we asked our guest editors—published authors and publishers—for feedback. Thirty-six selected pieces were then edited over the summer.

The writers in our first annual anthology share themes amplified by current events, but not the context. Stories of family, economic inequality, sexual violence, social justice, culture wars, lost love, aging, and gender—they're all in here. And mangoes. Everyone loves mangoes.

Luckily, I work with visionary educators who encouraged and helped our team to facilitate the production of the Anthology. Tip of the hat to Dr. Stephen Cohen, Dr. Melissa Mentzer, and the entire faculty and staff in the CCSU English department. A big thanks to Dr. Robert Wolff, Dean of the Carol A. Ammon College of Liberal Arts and Social Sciences and the senior CCSU administration—particularly the CCSU Foundation. Kudos to the good folks at the Connecticut Literary Festival and designer Jillian Goeler.

The contributors in this inaugural anthology hail from Windsor to Niantic, and Litchfield to Griswold. It's a diverse ensemble. Thank you to all the writers who trusted us with their work, and a hearty congratulations to the writers whose work you hold in your hands.

Jotham Burrello
September 2020

PANDEMIC: A LOVE POEM IN FOUR PARTS
B. FULTON JENNES

1

I wake early, draw back night-drenched drapes
so that when you rise
only brightness greets you.

I add milk and sugar to your cup,
you slice me a serving of coffee cake
twice as large as yesterday's.

We close cupboard doors left ajar
without complaint, extinguish lights
left blazing in empty rooms.

Our disquiet makes us indulgent,
reminds us that there may not always be
love to leave half-eaten.

2

A riot of yellow trumpets salutes
our passing as we amble to the lake.

You nod at them and say, *Oh, look:*
the for Cynthias are in bloom.

A gentle mondegreen, barely worth
correcting. Except I always do—

I've set you straight a score of years,
but today there are greater urgencies:

the startled *chip!* of a sanguine cardinal
that swoops across our path.

A blue sky, veined with brown branches
as we look to an expectant heaven.

The way our footsteps coincide in
silence, kiss the earth as if a single tread.

The amazement that we've walked
this far on a road that's never been

strewn with so much wonderment,
doused in so much light.

3

Spring repeats herself
like a babbling old fool,
asking again if lunch is ready.

She mutters in crocuses,
daffodils, shadblow—the same
beautifully bowed gifts

she has borne time and again—
mud and rain, mud and rain,
an endless reprise.

How is it that we adore her
now more than ever, like an elder
rooted in a shabby armchair

whose head we cannot help
but kiss with each passing,
although we endure

their endless mewling,
although we know that these
blossoms too will fade?

4

My mother's last words were
I want to walk in the rain
and feel the rain on my face

although she abhorred how
her bones ached, how her hair frizzed,
with the falling barometer.

Loss sharpens our senses,
makes us hungry for foods
we did not know we favored.

Our appetites now
betray how little we loved
what we love, before. 🛡️

BEYOND THE SEA
MARINA TINONE

O sangue frio de uma mãe. That's how Grandpa tells the story. Tio Luis was a kid and to prove to Grandpa he wasn't scared of heights, he climbed out onto the balcony and tried to *homem-aranhā* himself from one ledge to the other. I imagine my uncle, maybe eight or ten years old, grasping the outside railing of the balcony, his back to the open air, planning the best way to grasp the wall with only his hands and his feet. The Kida family lived in an apartment over ten floors up. What it took, according to Grandpa, for a mother to not scream out and to instead firmly grasp her child from behind the railing and pull him back to safety, was the cold blood of a mother.

I guess, in English, the expression would be *nerves of steel,* but I prefer the Portuguese. You have to be coolheaded to save your child. The writer Claudia Dey argues that mothers are the makers of death; the creation of life is also the creation of another death. I think you need something cold within you to truly realize it. You have to know death to preserve and love life. *Nerves of steel* sounds like a mechanical replacement; *sangue frio* makes the change total and permanent in your body. Besides, I like the way Grandpa tells the story so gravely: *o sangue frio de uma mãe*. Cold blood, something only mothers can have.

My mother, despite looking so much like Grandma, takes more after Grandpa in the rhythm of her voice, her gestures, her cautioning tone. I remember hearing Grandpa's seriousness in my mother, when I was little, at home in Connecticut: Nina—Mom always called me Nina—do you know what to do if you're caught in a riptide? You swim diagonally against it. You keep swimming, even if you're tired, you have to keep swimming against the riptide until you reach the end. That's why you swim diagonally—at some point, you have to find the end point. Then you're free. My mother had been caught in riptides when she was a kid growing up in Rio, Brazil. She wanted to make sure I knew how to save myself. Every time I entered the ocean water, I would tread the water cautiously, wondering if something would ever pull me back or into it. Nothing ever did, but at least I knew how to get out. I walked to shore and looked back at the sea. Maybe next time, it would, and Mom's words would come true. She named me Marina, *of the sea*, because of her love of the ocean. Maybe one day, I thought, I would really feel like I was part of the sea. I would feel my mother's ocean, the one she loved to reminisce about, the one with riptides.

Swimming in the ocean was the closest I ever experienced to flying. Or at least, as a kid, I had imagined that the buoyancy of the water would feel like the lift of the open sky. I had been on airplanes since I was three, flying from the States to family in Brazil; I have always known that the sky looked different from the ocean I swam in. But between the sky and the sea, I connected them. There's the famous bossa nova song, "Aquarela," that Mom taught me. From the moment I heard the lyrics *"Tanto céu e mar, um beijo azul,"* I knew this blue kiss was something real. I searched the horizon line for the meeting of those two expanses of blue, and I smiled.

I wanted to be like my mom. I wanted to love the ocean as much as she did. I already looked remarkably like her—my own brother mistook an old childhood picture of my mom with one of me—so I wanted to prove I was like her. She grew up a tomboy, so I wanted to be less girly. She could notice intricate patterns, fold origami with precise, sharp folds. I refolded and refolded the paper until it went soft in my hands. Still, I had kept trying. I only gave up trying to be her when I realized that I loved words more than she ever did. I gave up when I realized my childhood would never be hers. I knew when, on the flight back from Brazil, I would peer out the airplane window at the isolated suburbs below and search for deciduous New England forests that I called home. My eyes strained past the horizon line hoping for a glimpse. I would press my palm against the cold glass and watch the film of water spread around the heat of my hand and I would think, it's just like home. Just like the winter, when I would look out the window on a snowy day.

My birthday is in December. My relatives in Brazil would call me, one by one, to wish me happy birthday. They would ask if it was snowing because in Brazil, in the other hemisphere, it was summer, and they were having a barbecue or going to the beach. They would ask if I was going to go see them later that year, in August, when it would be my summer vacation and their winter. I didn't get to see them every year, but in the years my family did go to Brazil, my relatives would take me and my brother to the beach. In the dead of Brazil's winter, my brother and I spent hours in the water because even then, the Brazilian water was warmer than Connecticut's. The few other beachgoers would look at us and ask our parents sitting on the sand, What's wrong with your kids? The strangers were kind, of course, and they always asked the question jokingly, but they always expected a serious answer. Oh, we're visiting from the States, my mom would say before gesturing to us kids shouting in the water. They're American.

As an American, it took me a long time to get used to being Brazilian. From joking and friendly teasing between strangers, the slightest provocation when I was little would make me cry and in Brazil, I cried a lot. I made so many mistakes there: mixing up the names of my mother's many aunts, forgetting the names of family friends, lacking the know-how to eat certain tropical fruits, going blank when asked the simplest of questions, greeting people by kissing the wrong cheek (or worse, directly on the lips). But still, despite these faux-pas, I looked forward to Brazil. To be in a place, dare I call it a home, where everyone called me by the nickname my mother gave me. *Nina.* My whole family calls me by that name, their São Paulo accent hitting a nearly Italian cadence and enunciation.

But in America, I was Marina. Muhreenuh: the syllables slurred together so fast that my best friend, in kindergarten, spelled my name "Mrrena." At six years old, I was irked she had butchered my name so badly. But I choked back my indignation and thanked her for the card she had written me. I knew that my own love of words, even back then, was a personal thing. She wouldn't have understood. Eventually, classmates would mistake me for the other Asian girl in our school and call me by the wrong name entirely. After those instances, I stopped taking issue with people spelling my name wrong as long as I knew it was Marina they wanted to be with.

I never had a nickname in English. The closest one I ever got was given to me by the friend I made in the fourth grade. We would play make-believe and she would yell for me, "My-nuh! Mine-uh!" while she chased after me. I would run and answer, breathlessly, in another silly voice. We would laugh until our sides split from the running and our broken giggles. It was good to be ten years old when the only limit to our fun was the end-of-recess whistle. But even the whistle didn't stop us, not really. There were also long afternoons spent at her house, in the backyard, filming terrible comedy sketches and making arts and crafts.

One particular afternoon, we were playing on her swing, a simple plank of wood with a rope threaded through it. The rope itself was knotted to a steep-angled branch, meaning the swing rotated around the circumference of the tree. My friend wound the rope around the tree, ran diagonal to it, and jumped onto the seat of the swing, spiraling around the tree and hitting her back against the trunk. Now you try.

I was too scared to run and jump. It looked painful. I didn't want to get hurt, and I was too embarrassed to try only to catastrophically fail. I tried hiding my apprehension, but she noticed it anyway. What are you, a landlubber?

Even through my frustration, I thought, That's such a weird word. So American. I hated the idea that I was a landlubber, that I was unaccustomed to being at sea. What I hated more was that, through her inarticulacy, the word also sounded like *land-lover*. And I didn't want to prove that I had any sentimental attachment to the land, or to anything. I had too much pride. So I swallowed and wound the rope to an even tighter, even more precarious angle.

This friendship would later become fraught. But I didn't know that back then, when I planned my flight around the tree. I didn't know that this girl who was teaching me, at that moment, to be brave would later teach me to be scared. She would teach me, after her suicide attempt the next year, that life was precious. She would teach me to listen, and then to listen for dear life. She would teach me to hold her and attend to her jagged breathing after a panic attack. She would teach me that life was worth saving and that trying to save her life would come at the cost of both of our childhoods. I didn't know that, years later, I would have to pick up the pieces of myself that I had lost in the name of what I called our friendship. But again, I didn't know. What I did know, at least, was to still my breath, to calm down, to hold myself. In the fall air, sweat cooled on my forehead. I ran my diagonal and I jumped, knowing the air would catch me. ◈

SUNFLOWER MAZE
BENJAMIN S. GROSSBERG

From the viewing stand, we see ways out as giggly
families bumble through sunflowers.

Fieldside, we *were* suddenly in love
with sunflowers.

In the garden, rising from vines of hard-shell squash
like flaming torches: seven sunflowers.

I drive down to visit her and her damaged heart. Rigid
beside me, bloom on the headrest, a sunflower.

I say they speak to me, but the intimacy
is between sun and sunflower.

Faces beam, sun beams. Beams, also, the yellow-
petaled bloom of a sunflower?

Seed hive? Stasis chamber for hundreds in inter-
stellar sleep? What lodges in the disk of a sunflower?

Early spring, I'll crouch to rip out the kettle-
bell-dense roots of each sunflower.

O brash joining! The grooms' lapels match
golden cummerbunds with sunflowers.

Curves dull and hard like industrially molded
plastic: the back of each sunflower.

Hone neglect. Early watering breeds shallow
roots, and—timber!—there goes your sunflower.

I thought maybe—briefly—when he insisted
that we pull over to gaze at the field of sunflowers.

My boxes of photographs, diaries, birthday cards—
as practical as a harvest of sunflowers.

He did it to amuse me, the bud vase, the jamming,
the thick stalk of the sunflower.

Wanting you back, or a version that loved me, I imagine
leaving, like a pike across your door, a sunflower.

We take one in hand and spin, accelerating with
twirling ballast: the bloom of a sunflower.

Petal fall, birds launch at the disk, beaks puncturing,
hollowing each striated seed inside the sunflower.

Day one, balance a seed on your fingertip.
Day one hundred, stand in the shade of your sunflower.

Late at night, a neighbor sneaked into this garden
with a coping saw, canvas gloves, and a lust for sunflower.

Ben: son. Ben*jamin*: son of the right hand.
Their gay gardener, I answer also to Sunflower. ✦

MARY JOHNSON OF WETHERSFIELD, CONNECTICUT, HANGED FOR WITCHCRAFT, 1648

VIVIAN SHIPLEY

For over two hundred years, I was labeled the first witch
to be executed in the New World. Unlike Alse Young,
who was hanged May 26, 1647, my name was recorded.
I wish I had known her. We could have shared spells.

Dated December 7, 1648, there is only one sentence
about me in Connecticut records: "The jury finds
the Bill of Indictment against Mary Johnson that
by her own confession she is guilty of familiarity
with the Devil." They did not describe their test
of "watching and waiting," where I had to sit
with my legs crossed into an X for twenty-four hours.

I passed out and did not see the devil's familiar
judges said appeared to suck on my witch's teat
that they found by fingering my most private part.

I got better press in 1689 from Cotton Mather in
Memorable Providences: "She said, That a Devil
was wont to do her many services. Her Master
once blam'd her for not carrying out the Ashes,
and a Devil did clear the Hearth for her afterwards.
Her Master sending her into the Field, to drive out
the Hogs that us'd to break into it, a Devil would
scowre them out, and make her laugh to see
how he feaz'd 'em about." A servant girl, I was
first arrested for stealing and whipped for that crime
August 21, 1646, in Hartford and a month later
in Wethersfield. Naturally I was discontent and not
surprised when Satan eeled his way into me
for the first time. Sometimes he was winged, hooved,
or finned. Under my skin, he was alien yet familiar.

Yes, I had admitted to many unclean acts with
too many men I now label devils to remember.
No idea who the father might be, I had no choice
but to smother my newborn son, but unlike other
witches I knew, I never would eat flesh of a child
or use its fat to cast spells. I could cause a cow's milk
to dry up, corn crops to fail, cheese to turn sour.

In my confession I didn't mention I had the power,
with Satan's help, to steal a man's penis, make
genitals disappear so they could not be seen or felt.
I should have stored parts I removed in a box
or bird's nest where they could move and I could
feed them oats and corn. If I had not been in jail
while giving birth to a second son, I would have made
sure he was not bound out until he was twenty-one
as a servant to the jailer's son, Nathaniel, who took
fifteen pounds to take care of and educate the boy even
though there was a good chance he was his own child.

A tough man to please, Cotton Mather wrote
in *Magnalia Christi Americana*: "At her execution . . .
she went out of this world with many hopes
of mercy through the merit of Jesus Christ . . .
and she died in the frame [of mind] extremely
to the satisfaction of them that were spectators of it.
Our God is a great forgiver." By the rat's tail!
Hard to believe, but would a man of God lie? ◗

ADMIRAL IASKO DREAMS OF THE SEA
MIKA TAYLOR

Admiral Iasko's most cherished goal was to conquer some coastline—a bit of beach to call his own. He wasn't particular: just a spit with a harbor, a dock, and a clear path to the ocean. There, he could keep the decommissioned Borei submarine those Chechens had assured him was on its way.

The trouble started with the ice baths. Aleksey, the youngest and the admiral's cousin's son, had only ever lasted forty-five seconds underwater.

"Not again, Uncle."

For months, the admiral had been drilling the Royal Navy. His twenty men at arms practiced in the palace basement, executing maneuvers: dive, surface, silence, battle stations. The ship would need a crew of 107, but this core contingent could command. His chief, Drozd, stood alongside the pool.

"Get in," commanded Drozd.

"We won't be in water except to drown."

"In!" Drozd yelled.

"Let's just do the isolation drill. It's more realistic."

The men shifted. Aleksey wasn't wrong. In the sub, they'd be underwater, not in it.

Drozd shouted again, this time rapping his rifle on the ground.

The boy did not flinch.

"A hundred push-ups," said the admiral. "And then you run." All of them dropped, including Aleksey. Drozd had never known how to pick his battles.

"He weakens the chain of command," Drozd said. "If we're ever in a real submarine, his back talk will get us all killed."

The admiral couldn't tell if his men had heard. He gripped his pistol, a Makarov that had served him well.

"Laps!" he shouted. The men took off. The fall of their boots on the cement floor echoed through the space.

While he knew that he could not be questioned so openly without repercussion, the admiral didn't relish the prospect of bloodshed. The running of countries was no simple thing. With so many petty conflicts, a commander hardly had time to do what was right. All he had was loyalty and the brief flutter of control brought on by genuine fear and respect. The admiral had done much to become the leader he was and would willingly do worse, but none of that excited him anymore. Since the news of the submarine, he yearned only for the sea.

As the troops rounded the last corner, he drew his weapon.

"In," he said. The boy stopped cold. The rest jogged on. "Now."

Aleksey climbed into the ice bath without protest, panic in his eyes. It calmed the admiral, who clicked his stopwatch. Fifteen seconds passed, then twenty.

"This navy will not stand insubordination!" Drozd yelled to the others as they ran. "An officer's word is law!"

Fifteen seconds, thirty.

The men rounded back toward them. Thirty-five seconds,

forty. When they got close, the admiral cocked his pistol and wondered if, beneath the water, the boy heard it click.

Forty-five seconds, fifty. Without taking his eyes from the watch, Admiral Iasko swung his arm to the right and loosed a bullet into Drozd's head. He felt the familiar kick in his shoulder, but the rest of him was still. There was no pleasure in the moment, no rush of power. His chief crumpled. Aleksey sunk deeper into the icy water. The men picked up their pace, veering only slightly to avoid the fallen body, the spreading delta of brains and blood. He'd make Aleksey clean it up later. Fifty-five seconds, sixty.

He didn't need a long beach, or a beautiful one, just enough to launch from. Any small spit would be sufficient. Or an island maybe. Yes, even an island would do. 🜂

MOM WAITING FOR THE BUS ON THE CORNER OF PAVILION AND MAIN

MELISSA MCEWEN

"Why you always gotta be so mad?" / I got a lot to be
mad about.

—Solange

Though her insides are cotton
soft like the summer dress she's wearing
she can't be all-the-way tender or all-the-way happy
because her babies are black and male, with skin

soft like the summer dress she's wearing.
She knows the world won't see them, love them like she does
because her babies are black and male with skin
people will always see first. Black before human.

She knows the world won't see them, love them like she does.
She knows the outcome:
people will always see first—black before human.
She prays hard and turns down the sound when the news is on.

35

She knows the outcome.
She's tired of hearing that another black boy was shot.
She prays hard and turns down the sound when the news is on.
Her friend just told her a boy was shot on Bedford.

She's tired of hearing that another black boy was shot
by police or in a drive-by or stabbed over something stupid.
Her friend just told her a boy was shot on Bedford.
It's no wonder why she's mad. Black boys are shot

by police or in a drive-by or stabbed over something stupid.
She can't be all-the-way tender or all-the-way happy.
It's no wonder why she's mad (black boys are shot)
though her insides are cotton. ♠

CHARLOTTE
JOSÉ B. GONZÁLEZ

my uncle's parrot
    did this dip,
        a dance,
dropped her neck
        toward
          seeds
like each bite
    she took was what
was due,
like she should
be paid
    for living in a cage.

I try to tell Mrs. C. that someone
should write a book about that bird,
that dance,
    that dip,
and she belly laughs as we continue

reading about Wilbur the pig, survival
in the barn, and Charlotte the spider
that lived on a web by the door, how
she warned the pig when it got close
that death would be close to the door.

I wanted to tell Mrs. C. that my uncle's
parrot has a dance for death too, that she
doesn't warn when it comes but that she
flaps   her wings
                          after it leaves,
that she makes
        this wind that carries
                    dirt into your eyes, that
I saw her build gusts so strong that they
could knock down barns.

By the time we reach
                    the last page,
the spider is gone. I say, Mrs. C.,
if the parrot had been Charlotte,
                she would
                          still be flapping, she
would have ripped
                the flap off the book
if only she had lived
inside the pages,

but Mrs. C. just tells me that I'm missing
the symbols, but she's missing how I'm just
missing the cousins
        whose bodies are cold,
                how they used to dance. ◆

MULLING SPICES
SITARA GNANAGURU

I don't really cook, yet
I crave to paint the palate
with a palette of spices, master
my native cuisine.

I hunger for Ammachi's taste
and talent in the kitchen,
to know just how to stir the pot—
until the aroma awakens the sleeper
within:

a girl in tune with her
Tamil roots, who won't mask
her ethnicity with quiet,
unassuming blandness.

I'm desperate to feed my lack,
satisfy my memory,
nourish my soul.

If home cooking is a kind
of magic, and recipes
are spells, then

let saffron stain my disposition
sunny; turmeric trigger
tenacity; clove, cinnamon,
and cardamom massage
enough sweetness to temper
tamarind; and bay leaf be
a balm, bringing it all home.

Lest I lose my way,
I'll leave myself
a trail of mustard
seeds and black
Peppercorns.

A SINKING FEELING
MAKENZIE OZYCZ

The teenage swim instructor bellows from a distance, "Approach the diving board, feet together!"

Step one. Step two. Step three. Step four. Plant feet. Look out. Blue. Blue. Blue.

The toxic smell of chlorine stings the inside of my nose. The sound of dozens of wet feet scuttling along monotonous glossy-blue ceramic radiates through my eardrums. I'm disgusted by this place. Small, crescent-moon fingernail indents decorate my sweaty palms. Frantic, I look left to right, the neon posters making my eyes squint:

No Running.

Lifeguard on Duty at All Times.

A red rope linked with reflective buoys separates the shallow end from the deep. The thin rope wavers loosely in the water as the other kids zoom around and beneath it. Nobody is going to save them if they begin to sink under the water. They're just another bobbing buoy in a sea of twenty-odd eight-year-olds. Just keep your head above the water. Hold your nose.

Don't open your eyes. Unlike them, maybe I just never took direction well.

The court clerk commands. "Approach the bench, raise your right hand."

Step one. Step two. Step three. Step four. Plant feet. Look out. Narrow eyes. Evil smirk.

The truth. The whole truth. Nothing but the truth.

My small, shaking voice escapes through bitten, chapped lips and at first, I don't even recognize it as my own. It sounds pathetic. Scared. Nervous. Like that of a little girl trapped at the deep end of the swimming pool. I start to sink into myself, sink down, down, down. I'm being pulled, memories like currents, currents like cinder blocks tied to my ankles.

My weak lungs let out small sighs as the public defender pushes on. Frantic, I lose my voice. He continues to push: "You're lying. Where's the proof? You're a seriously disturbed girl, aren't you?" I'm a liar, I have no proof, I'm a seriously disturbed girl.

The swim instructor continues to push. "Jump off, Makenzie. Jump."

I idle, inhale, squeeze shut my eyes, and jump. Immediate panic overtakes my every sense. My legs fail the rest of my body, my arms aren't fast enough for my brain, the surface is too far away, the water too cold, my floaters too deflated. Help. Help. Help? Nothing.

The public defender pushes on. "Could it be you drank too much that night?"

I watch the condensation run slowly down the glass of water to my left like sap on a tree stump. I run my finger against it. I wipe the moisture from my hand onto my lap. I look up. I look back down. I unclench my fists. The crescent moon fingernail imprints decorate my sweaty palms. I pick up the glass. It almost slips from my grasp. The water inside ripples.

I imagine it consuming me. It's in my lungs. It's drowning my organs. I look ahead. I look for help. Help. Help. Help? Nothing.

"You have to test yourself! Get back in the pool."

Chlorine stings my bloodshot eyes. My throat is dry from deep sobs escaping amid hyperventilation. I'll never swim again. I look out. Twenty-odd eight-year-olds dance before me like raindrops on hot summer sidewalks. I look down at myself. My shimmering pink one-piece and black-and-purple water shoes mock me. Maybe I will swim again. I drop the towel. I walk to the edge. I look down, past my feet, past the "4 ft" painted in large black strokes on the side of the pool, right into the water. It ripples as the other kid's splash.

"Listen, girls lie about this stuff all the time."

Twenty-something strangers sit in the rows of the courtroom staring blankly ahead. They bob like buoys: heads up, heads down, looking left, looking right. A sea of strangers and one shark. He smirks at me. I clench my fists. I stare at my hands. I start to feel a current drag me under. I don't speak, the water in the glass to my left crowds my lungs. I begin to choke. I cough, I breathe, I look out in front of me, I see my friends, I see my family, I see the surface. I sip the water again. I clear my throat. I smirk back.

The swim instructor tries to reason. "Every little girl gets taught how to swim."

I sit on the ledge. I let my feet make small tsunamis in the shallow end of the swimming pool and turn my back on the instructor. When I get up, I take one stair at a time until half my body is submerged in the lukewarm, turquoise-tiled shallow end. I see the other kid's jump, carefree, from the diving board; like pennies dropped off skyscrapers they almost disappear before hitting the surface of the water and magically popping back up through the waves seconds later. I'm not there yet.

I'm not like the other twenty-something eight-year-olds. But someday, I will be.

The public defender attempts to rationalize. "My defendant comes from a good family. He's an A student. He has no priors. He's a good kid."

Except for when he did this.

And again when he did that.

And when he left this scar on my right arm.

And called twenty-something times in one day, all sent to voice mail.

I start slowly and find my voice. Then, I dive in headfirst. The words escape fast yet steady like synchronized swimmers pushing off from the back of a swimming pool. Maybe I don't know any good techniques. Maybe I'm learning as I go. But I swim like they do, and I swim. I don't stop until there's no more air left in my lungs and no more words left on my tongue. When I stop, I feel myself floating for a moment. Then, I firmly plant myself. I'm no longer nervous, no longer scared, no longer pathetic. The courtroom is silent. Tears fall down my face like condensation droplets rolling down the glass of water to my left.

The swim instructor applauds me. "I didn't think you had it in you!"

Fourteen years later, I sit at the edge of the pool. I'll never be a professional diver, but I've conquered this place. That lethal chlorine wafts through the air, everything looks and feels smaller when you're suddenly much bigger. The diving board, no more than five feet off the ground, no longer holds dominion over my once-anxious mind. As I leave, I watch a crowd of kids rush onto the glossy blue ceramic, like a school of fish ready to leap into the deep end. I smile as I think about eight-year-old me, resisting free swim in her shimmering pink one-piece and purple-and-black water shoes.

My lawyer pats my shoulder as I return to my seat. "I didn't think you had it in you."

The shark sneers at me through jagged teeth. Eight years and no probation. Case closed. I think back to childhood, then to the pool. Jump, Makenzie, jump. But if I jump when I'm not ready, what's the point? So I jump when I am. I jump when I realize life isn't always fair to little girls whose biggest problem is learning how to swim. When I realize sharks are real, and they come in all shapes and sizes. And when I jump now, the waves surround me. They no longer suffocate me. And I swim: for my friends, for my family, for other girls, but mostly, for me. 🐚

RADAR
CECILIA GIGLIOTTI

It's rather an unassuming place
To shelter the best of the human race:
A sharp pair of ears, or a nervous face.

It's quite an inopportune time to learn
The manifold ways a man can burn—
But you're young, and taught to wait your turn.

It's easy for these things to leave their mark.
It's always been less of a walk in the park
Than a blind sort of stumble, a shot in the dark.

It's the constant vision, vivid as chrome:
A hundred souls bleeding, their mouths frothing foam,
And you can go back but you cannot go home.

It's not just a question of what you know,
But how many lives it can save; and so
You're poised on the tip of your tongue, your toe.

It's only for you to manage affairs,
To look in the face of death as it stares,
To hear, and to never be caught unawares.

So it's one step ahead, one second before,
An uncanny knack for predicting the score,
Making a farm boy a man of war. ♟

FAIR LAWN, NEW JERSEY: 1997
KATHERINE A. SZPEKMAN

We are passing the bagel store
and you are strapped in your car seat.
You can't be more than three.
Sun floods the green station wagon
and wraps us like a golden fur
this fall morning, when everything is new,
and your hands are so small.

Mama. Look at the leaves and the trees and the blue sky,
you chant, swinging your legs,
red leotards bunched at the ankles.
I drive behind sunglasses,
and in the time it takes to dart my eyes
to the rearview mirror

and back, you ask, Mama, why do we die?
More a song you make up
than a question,
the ache to cup my mouth
upon yours, breath
apple-juice sweet,

to inoculate you,
promise you everything,
believe I am magic,
forged from cast iron,
an eternal vessel
to hold you, even when I am gone.

But I know this moment
is a thumbtack on our map,
a stain I can't remove.
And the illusion of protection
is a charade, weightless
as it slips through my fingertips

like your silky brown hair
through a fine-tooth comb,
a first death.
Later, I will feed you lunch
in the big yellow kitchen,
your tiny fingers wrapped
around a peanut butter sandwich. ♦

WELCOME ABOARD THE GARRETT BRIGGS CAMPAIGN

KATHRYN FITZPATRICK

Please read and sign this form to acknowledge that everything we're going to review in this orientation tour is confidential, officially.

Your internship began at approximately 7:37 a.m. today and will end at 9:55 p.m. the day after the election. I must remind you that this job is completely unpaid, you will be required to work a minimum of six fourteen-hour days per week, and there is no mileage reimbursement, no travel reimbursement, no health-care reimbursement, no dry-cleaning reimbursement.

Yes, there is a dead body on the table used by mailing campaign volunteers. Yes, that is real blood soaking the forever stamps. Today, the volunteers will be cleaning those stamps and drying them in the windows facing the Aldi's parking lot.

Though you are unpaid, you are not a volunteer. You are an intern, which entitles you to a handsome form letter recommendation signed by the senator once you have completed your internship.

You are entitled to order a latte for yourself on every other coffee run you make. That's approximately eighteen coffee runs per week, which equals nine lattes for you, so, if you purchase the most expensive of the seasonal lattes at the largest size (which I don't suggest you do, unless you want Denise to take it out of the budget for your welcome party and your going-away party—which means oatmeal cookies instead of cupcakes, which means disappointed coworkers, which means vegetable oil in your gas tank), this means the Garrett Briggs campaign is officially unofficially paying you $5.95 per every other coffee run or $53.55 per week.

The dead body was the last intern. Her name was Amber.

I must also remind you that you were chosen from a highly competitive group of candidates. Mostly out-of-work campaign managers and law school graduates with immense student load debt. This does not make you special. But enjoy the moment.

Yes, that is a purple mitten in the mouth of the intern-now-dead-body Amber.

She was accepted into the internship program over more qualified candidates because Senator Briggs wanted more diversity on the staff and Amber was the only one who wore purple mittens to the interview. Anxiety, probably.

This is my office. If the door is shut, do not knock. If the door is open, buzz me through the intercom phone first, wait ten seconds, and if I do not answer, hang up and wait thirty minutes before trying again.

Finding Amber's killer has jumped up to third on my list of priorities, behind your orientation and drafting sixteen separate press releases detailing the senator's stance on four different topics on which he has not yet decided his stance.

Yes, Amber is wearing a graphic T-shirt with a depiction

of Naugatuck, Connecticut. After killing her, someone painted a red X on it, stuffed the mitten in her mouth, and wrote #BriggsBabe in black Sharpie on her right arm. Maybe it means something, but maybe not. Most things do not. Do not get lost in the details.

This is your desk. This is your stapler. This is your computer. This is your penholder. Pens are kept in the supply closet around the corner, as are computer paper, highlighters, tissues, tampons, mouthwash, boxes of staples, and so on. Please only take one pen at a time. When you take supplies, please note what you take on the supply chart on the wall on the right. Senator Briggs gives a breakdown of all campaign expenses to his most valuable donors. Scrupulous questioners. Retired.

I do not think they killed Amber. They never would have let blood soak the forever stamps in such a way. Wasteful.

This is your phone. Do not answer the phone if the call is coming through on lines two through seven. Line one, you may answer, but only if it is a high-pitched ring. If it is low pitched, let Sandra answer. Low pitch means the call is coming from a wealthy home.

The woman who wears sweater vests is Sandra. Sandra handles all relations with wealthy benefactors. She may not be much to look at, but she has a way on the phone. She works around the clock and takes only six twenty-minute naps a day. Do not stare directly into Sandra's eyes—direct eye contact makes her freeze up for the better part of twenty-four hours. That is twenty-four hours of phone donations we lose. If you look directly into her eyes, a committee will determine how much revenue was lost and that will come out of your paycheck (i.e., lattes).

Sandra was frozen until approximately three minutes before your arrival. Amber was killed last night. Senator Briggs himself looked Sandra right in the eye yesterday morning after a particularly stern staff meeting where the senator expressed frustration with the lack of negative ads being used against his opponents. He bought us plain doughnuts with no frosting or sprinkles in protest. He made Amber and Marsha pose with him for a series of Instagram photos. The caption read "Young people are our future. Young women have a voice." Along those lines.

Daryl shared the photos on Twitter and Facebook but was not happy about it.

You'll meet Daryl and Marsha in a minute. You've already met Amber, though she's not really herself today—a bit drained, I'd say.

That was a joke. You may laugh—this time.

You will have to be creative to get Sandra's attention without catching her eye. I've found that throwing single staples at the ceramic planter next to her desk usually gets her attention. I have great aim. I pitched for the senator's softball team two years in a row. If you have never pitched softball before, I suggest you find a different method. Staples go rogue. And when they go rogue, they land on the floor near Rusty's office.

There are staples lodged in the back of Amber's calves, which suggests she was dragged across the floor near Rusty's office.

That is Rusty, the senator's graphic designer. Rusty makes the senator look hip, like the face of the future.

Rusty walks around the office barefoot. He was treated for rage issues for many years and only recently went off his meds on the condition he stick to a strict regime of meditation, yoga, and a movement called barefoot romanticism. He does this to inhale the purest spiritual air. Believe me, you do not want to see what happens when Rusty steps on a staple and does not get his required amount of spiritual air.

Rusty does not create the negative ads against the senator's opponent. That is also part of his strict regime. So Tim creates the negative ads.

The senator hired Tim after details leaked about the senator's trip to Mexico last spring. The senator also decided to stop going to Mexico for his weekend trips and now goes to Naugatuck, Connecticut.

Tim is Senator Briggs's nephew. He rides a scooter and does most research using Wikipedia. He has created one negative campaign in nine weeks. The claims in the commercial could only be attributed to a Wiki user named BriggsBabe69 and no supporting evidence could be found.

Tim is in love with Madelynn, but they don't talk. That is Madelynn at the desk by the storage closet. She handles email marketing and is very good at asking for money through email. This means she is very good at eliciting sympathy, guilt, and sense of duty.

Last week, Madelynn consulted with beggars in the Instagram holding tank about how they could integrate email-based fundraising into their efforts and signed them all up for free Mailchimp accounts. She and Rusty previously taught free classes on individual fundraising and spiritual fulfillment.

This beggar was the first recruit for the Instagram room. Amber was in charge of the senator's Instagram account and, upon seeing the need for constant photos with homeless people, babies, young Republican mothers, people in wheelchairs, and anyone vaguely "ethnic" looking, Amber decided the most efficient thing would be to keep some of these people on retainer.

The Instagram holding room is next to the supply closet. If you borrow a beggar, please sign him or her out on the form by the door.

Madelynn is a lesbian, but we are not supposed to know that. We did not seat her by the closet on purpose for some cruel sense of irony. Officially, we do not know she is gay.

Madelynn is the senator's illegitimate daughter. She does not know this. Tim does not know this. Officially, neither do we.

Amber knew this. The senator told her on a visit to Naugatuck, Connecticut, unofficially.

The senator has not made an official announcement as to his official feelings on homosexual marriage, officially. It is best to be able to claim ignorance of her lesbianism in case it turns out the senator is against gay marriage or homosexuals in general, whatever happens to be the best argument at the time.

In the center of the office is the social media desk. Daryl is Twitter and Facebook. There is an empty seat at his desk. That is where Amber sat. She was in charge of Instagram and Snapchat. They were in charge of exciting the younger generation.

Daryl used to date Marsha. Marsha does strategic planning for debates that the senator usually calls in sick for. Her desk is by the watercooler but she prefers coffee. The coffee maker is near the senator's office door, over there. When Marsha dated Daryl, she was useless. Now she is on fire. Daryl unfollowed her the day she dumped him.

Marsha dumped Daryl in order to have an affair with the senator. We don't know this, officially.

Marsha offered a few tidbits about the senator to Daryl that would humanize the senator. Things for him to share on social media. Personal things. How he likes his pancakes in the morning. How he sleeps with a teddy bear. How he reads *Goodnight Moon* every night.

Amber suggested a few others. Sexual positions. Music tastes. The mole in the center of his back.

These suggestions went ignored, unofficially.

Over there is the bulletin board where you're free to post personal flyers. Please do not post human body parts on the board. The killer cut out a small piece of Amber's heart and pinned it up by the Girl Scout cookie sign-up sheet. Cliché, if you ask me. Nothing original being said there. Hearts breaking and such.

To review: Daryl loves Marsha. Marsha loves the senator. Tim loves Madelynn, who is an unofficial lesbian and his unofficial cousin.

Tim doesn't have a desk. He prefers to be "migratory." He works on his scooter. Tim confessed his feelings to Madelynn at the office party two weeks ago. His advances were rejected, as Madelynn was in love with Amber. I heard the smacking of lips in the storage closet, unofficially.

There are only two things that can be deduced from the smacking of lips: kissing, or that a person has eaten something particularly delicious, which I know is not true. It was a potluck, after all.

The bathrooms are to the right. Those bloody boot marks with the clumps of loose staples are usually not there. Water coolers are to the left.

Tim and Daryl were caught stapling Amber's favorite beggar to a chair. The chair still has a bloodstain on the right arm. The beggar is sitting there now. Daryl was still angry about Marsha, who was angry that Amber had also recently slept with the senator. Madelynn was sulking in the corner because she, too, had heard that Amber was a #BriggsBabe.

Unofficially that is the title given to all women and men who sleep with the senator.

If it turns out the senator supports gay marriage, then we will throw Madelynn a party or get her a gift basket or however you handle such things.

Here is your invitation to Amber's funeral. There will be no discussing of Amber's sexuality at the funeral. She was not kissing Madelynn. She was not in bed with the senator. She helped beggars.

That is Denise. She wears a wig to disguise her bald head. Everyone knows it is a wig, so do not pretend like it is real hair. Many assumed she was bald because she had cancer and was going through chemotherapy.

Denise did not, in fact, have cancer. When her husband left her, she shaved her head and took a vow of silence for three months. No one noticed the silence.

The senator has no official stance on the war or when we should evacuate the troops. He does, however, support the troops.

Here is the copy machine. There is the beggar trying to choke Daryl. There is Tim taking photos of Amber for Facebook and the press and Instagram.

And here is Senator Briggs's office. There is blood on the doorknob and the carpet.

Tim will write the official story, which will go to press later this morning: Amber was killed by the senator's opponent, who set out to frame him as a sexual deviant, as a corrupter of the youth. Naugatuck, Connecticut. Mitten Mouth. #BriggsBabe.

It will be useful for you to know how to remove bloodstains from the carpet in the senator's office. And from his shirt. The senator has no official stance on this death, except that it is sad. Losing young people is never easy.

Pulls at the heartstrings. Mothers, sisters, fathers, brothers.

The senator is in his office now, staring out his window toward the Aldi's parking lot.

There are many things you can say about the senator, but the one thing no one disputes is that he is very handsome and very American looking. Especially when he perfects that tear-soaked look, that heart-broken silence in his eyes.

That just might win us the election. 🐾

OLD MAN WINTER
AVERY JENKINS

Leaning on the handle of the maul, I eyeball the woodpile sitting in front of me. We are both morosely sandwiched somewhere between fall's rowdy exuberance and spring's gentle murmurings, and I'm deliberating the wood's recent reappearance in my life. It had been hidden beneath a sizable pile of gray snow until a bout of warmer temperatures and rain exposed the upper half.

My winter-remaining-versus-wood-already-split calculations left a gap that would only be closed by an abnormal early spring or the addition of more wood under the deck. Not choosing to gamble on the former, I grabbed my maul and headed out back. Nobody likes a cold house in March.

It is a quintessential late New England winter afternoon. Sullen clouds sit above the trees, outlining the dark, leafless tree limbs below them. I stand at the bottom of a gravel driveway, now half-mud and half-ice, bound at the end by the dirty pile of snow with the last remaining row of unsplit wood poking out.

It feels cold, but a half-hearted cold. The biting, challenging cold of January is nowhere to be seen. A sweatshirt is sufficient outerwear, though I decided against the kilt, primarily because of the depth of the snow I would have to clamber through to get to my wood.

Winter's getting old, I think.

I heft the maul. So am I.

I grabbed my least favorite eight-pound maul. It's just a touch too heavy to wield for the longer splitting session I had in mind for the afternoon and lacks the finesse of my six-pound maul. But the handle of the six-pounder has gotten a bit too dry this winter, and the head wobbles to the extent that I'm sure I'll leave it buried deep in the maw of some slightly split piece of stringy wood, leaving me to flail about with wooden handle and frustration.

I wish I'd remembered to let the six-pounder soak in a bath of neat's-foot oil overnight, but I hadn't. That would have firmed the loose head right up. The eight-pounder, though, is equipped with a fiberglass handle that must be attached to the head with some sort of NASA space glue, because nothing I have ever done to it has even so much as loosened things. And I've managed to behead virtually every handled tool in existence, from a double-bit ax to a pick-mattock.

As it turned out, the bigger maul was the right call. At this point, I'm splitting wood a little past it's prime. Not yet punky, but dried past the point where grain has much governance over the split. Frozen as it is, when hit by a blast from Big Boy the Maul, the wood explodes into two or even three parts, making me feel like a cross between Paul Bunyan and the Terminator. Pieces fly several feet before landing, and I secretly hope someone is watching my display of lumber prowess.

Nobody is, though, except for the puppy, who comes out to visit and request a piece of split wood to chew on, and the birds hiding in the bushes, having their presupper conversations at an exuberant volume. It is that chatter as much as anything else that tells me that, although spring may not yet be here, winter's strength is waning and his power fading. A month ago, the birds were largely silent, conserving every ounce of energy for the enormous task of keeping warm and staying alive. I'm not anxious to see old winter go like most New Englanders. For those of us outside the cities, winter brings his own pleasures along with his trials. Few memories are as strong for me as drinking my morning coffee next to a flaming woodstove, feeling its heat ripple past me to the rest of the house. Those silent moments are a treasure.

Without warning, the birds' chatter silences as a cold north wind kicks up. Winter's assertion that maybe he's not as old as I think he is. Well, neither am I, for that matter. I ignore the sudden temperature drop, splitting a few more logs to reach my goal of bringing the woodpile even with the top of the snow. That'll teach winter who's the boss.

After splitting, I ferry a dozen or so wheelbarrows of split wood and stack it under the porch, where I hope it will dry out enough to be useful for me by the time I need it. I lean the wheelbarrow against the wood and go back to retrieve the maul. Picking it up, I feel the muscles in my back. They aren't sore, and they probably won't be, but they've been used enough to feel wanted and loved.

I look one last time to the low clouds of a stale winter sky. They still aren't talking.

I turn to go inside.

It's been a good afternoon with Old Man Winter. ⚜

SEASON OF GHOST APPLES
GINNY LOWE CONNORS

The gustnado was a surprise, coming as it did after a few fine days of Indian summer. Spinning and spinning leaves, twigs, and dirt into a spiral that stretched up and spread out in a thick, harsh swirl, it called the darkening sky down. Huge clouds. Hard, cold rain. Not a month later the ground seemed to explode, booming and banging—frost quakes. Icy groundwater freezing, expanding, pressing at rocks below. The ground popped like gunfire, and the sound boomeranged. Then, after days of gray weather: Thunder sleet. Rain turned to bullets of ice that pinged hard on the windows and clattered on the ground. The sky let loose with thunder and lightning that had no business arriving uninvited and unannounced—summer was long over. It was loud, crazy loud. Tree branches and sidewalk iced up. A strange landscape. Later, of course, came the bombogenesis, a blizzard that buried the state and kept on going. Trees down, power out, snow so high even the plows couldn't get through. Second night, the wind died down, though it kept on snowing. The world suddenly went quiet. What country was this? What

century? And how would it all be remembered? A painting, an
opera, an ornament?

icy spheres left behind
frozen apples turn to mush
slip through the crystalline globes—
ghost apples in the orchard 🛡

WAYWARD IN THE BLOOD
STEVEN OSTROWSKI
(For Tom Sullivan)

Hey Sul, we were brothers back then, geniuses
at the reservoir, obliterated but not once drowned.
Strung out and guitar minded, we laughed
where girls wouldn't go.

We estranged Staten Island, blurred all its yellow lines.
I grubbed for cigs and you grinned at my Ginsbergian poems.
Seventeen, you drove a Dodge Dart and I walked a lot.
We spent brain cells in bars, wasted wishes
on hot girls who found us hysterical but not quite.

Sul, one summer we thumbed and middle fingered our way
across America, remember? But it was those black-eyed
Native dudes in Minnesota who got a piece of historical revenge
when they took our money and didn't come back with the goods.

We tried to fish Hemingway out of the Big Two-Hearted River
but Papa fought us like a son of a bitch,
so we waded in without poles just to feel the clean copper cool
of a river that didn't ooze with Jersey oil.

West, we ascended into rocky space like grimy seraphim.
We fell asleep on switchbacks. We were skinny as tree line pines,
our songs had no radio, our hair was dirt-long but shampooed
by the sexy fingertips of the sun.

Way up on Longs Peak, we reflected weird in a pair of mountain girls'
azure eyes. We grinned a "Hey" and watched their beauty descend
giggling from the summit. Their loss, we laughed, ha ha, their loss,
and we headed down, headed home, thin soled and undefiled yet again,
headed east to figure ourselves into the rest of our lives.

Yo, Sul, you think those years of lust and rebel and howl
left some trace of wayward in our blood for good? I do. Now
and then I wonder how you've been. I hope you're aging
with a grace that's smoky and fierce. I don't imagine
you ever gave in. Me, I'm still writing my gravel and dust poems.
For who? I couldn't say. Doesn't matter. I know this for sure:
I'm doing what I want to do. 🛡

FINAL REGARDS FROM THE
BROTHERS PERRETTA
JEAN P. MOORE

What is it then between us?
What is the count of the scores or hundreds of years
between us?

Whatever it is, it avails not—distance avails not, and
place avails not . . .
—Walt Whitman, "Crossing Brooklyn Ferry"

Walking along the Bay of Naples, with Vesuvius in the distance, I see my shadow on ancient rocks, just as my ancestors once did. Our shapes in shadows, evidence of our lives. I've come to Naples to feel closer to those no longer casting shadows anywhere on this earth. Their hometowns are nearby where they lived as children before making the crossing, becoming Americans, and forgetting everything about their pasts, or, at least, trying to forget. Of course, that is not possible. Their history is held in the blood of the children. And so we live our lives, this blood whispering to us, telling us things we hardly understand. Yet, the stories will be told because, until then, there is no rest.

It is the story of my great-uncles Erasmo and Giuseppe Perretta that pulses.

In his cell, Erasmo prepares to write his letter to Governor Marcus H. Holcomb. I picture him sitting down at a small wooden table pushed up against the back wall of his cell. High above him is a barred window that, during the day, lets in only a small ray of sunlight. Now, a bare electric bulb screwed into the socket in the ceiling dimly lights the room. In twenty-four hours, Erasmo and Giuseppe will climb Eli Giddings's hanging machine. Erasmo has been trying to hide his fear, but he is growing frantic after exhausting all legal remedies, all appeals, all pleas. He must remain calm. He must focus on the task at hand: the letter.

A stack of prison paper sits before him on the desk. There are very specific rules about its use at the top of the first page. Write only on ruled lines. The inmate must confine himself to family or business of his own. Erasmo knows he will write many pages. There is so much to be said, so many injustices, so many things presented incorrectly. He must make the governor understand. This letter is his last chance to be heard.

He smooths the writing paper against the rough surface of the desk and picks up the fountain pen the guard has given him. He carefully dips it into the inkwell. Using his fingernail to pull the lever away from the barrel, Erasmo watches the bubbles form as the black ink is absorbed into the two little holes in the nib.

The guard watches to be certain the pen does not become a weapon. Erasmo thinks, let this pen be my sword.

His heart is beating fast, as it did the night of his arrest. If

Governor Holcomb is an honorable man, he will see, by this letter, that two brothers have been falsely accused.

Erasmo writes tentatively—he wants no mistakes. The pen makes its first marks, a number one with a raised, small zero next to it, underlined twice in the middle of the first line. Erasmo pauses. This first mark is good, written in a steady hand. He is not an educated man, but he is writing to His Excellency so the writing must be clean and neat. Erasmo must use proper language; he cannot use the dialect of his village. The interpreter who will prepare the letter in English for His Excellency must see that Erasmo is not a peasant, but a man with a trade, a shoemaker, with a home and a business of his own, with a wife and three babies. Erasmo and his brother are not murderers. Erasmo must make the interpreter, the Honorable Governor Holcomb, and anyone who will read this letter, see the brothers' innocence.

Your Excellency, Governor Holcomb:

I have decided to write this fateful letter regarding the unexpected, cruel sentence inflicted upon us, the innocent. Your Excellency, Governor, if what we write does not seem true, it is because they have made you understand that we are very murderous. We assure you we are two innocent men and that our death sentence is based on all lies inflicted upon us. We were in bed when this happened. Your Excellency, Governor Holcomb. Don't give your permission to make us two innocent victims. Be brave. Do everything you can to give us a new process, without injustice.

Your Excellency, Governor Holcomb, make an investigation and you will find that Frank Palmese, the victim, did not say "Erasmo shot me and Giuseppe cut

69

me." There were two nurses present who can tell you the truth.

Your Excellency, Governor Holcomb, on the morning of June 3, 1918, my house was surrounded and the officers who entered declared that I was under arrest, demanding if I knew anything about their questions, but I knew nothing of their questions because a man who sleeps knows nothing of what happens in the streets. Then my brother and I were handcuffed and taken to the hospital.

The injured man was lying on the bed deprived of his senses, and he supposedly gets Erasmo by the arm and says, "He shot me and Giuseppe cut me."

Your Excellency, Governor Holcomb, the interpreter asked him if he knew us; and Frank Palmese responded yes. And the interpreter asked him again if he had any quarrel with us, and Palmese said no.

Who will protect us from these lies?

Also, I have seen in the court, policemen who were never in my house, and yet they were on the stand testifying as if they had been there. And yet, the one officer who was at my house, Officer Dolan, was not in court. Why wasn't he allowed to testify? Because he would have told the truth, that he was the only one on night duty, on the beat, and at my house that night, and with his own mouth told me, "Don't worry, from 10:30 p.m. tonight, I have not seen you in the street." And this is all true, because anyone can tell you Officer Dolan was on the beat that night, and he can tell you what I am saying now.

This shows we were all framed up.

Your Excellency, Governor Holcomb, I again beg you; use all your influence; don't let two brothers die so cruelly. Someday, Your Excellency, Governor Holcomb, our innocence will be discovered and made known. Then it will be too late.

You will know all if you investigate.

Final regards from the brothers Perretta.

His letter goes on for many pages. Erasmo knows what he wants to say, that the judicial system is determined against him and his brother and has been from the start.

On June 9, 1919, the board of pardons hears the brothers' plea to have their death sentence commuted to life in prison. The brothers' counsel brings the case for commutation forward. They argue on the flimsiness of the circumstantial case, the insufficient evidence, the weak motive, and the ignored eyewitness testimony.

The state's position, as set forth by the prosecuting attorney, argues that the defense had never before questioned the evidence. "Besides," he proclaims, "as both brothers are anarchists, the state does not require a decided motive for the killing." He goes on to exhibit pistols and knives and steel-jacketed cartridges that miraculously appeared in the brothers' home on Cherry Street in New Britain the night of the murder—*after* the brothers had been whisked away, under arrest. No pistols, knives, or cartridges had been found during the initial search, when the brothers had been at home. The board of pardons rules against the brothers.

On June 27, 1919, at midnight, the death sentence is upheld.

Erasmo's widow, Amelia, stayed in New Britain with her babies. She stayed in their house and took in boarders. The house and shoe repair shop on Cherry Street gave way to the major highway that runs through the old Italian quarter. Amelia, who lived to be ninety-four, and her children with Erasmo have all died. No one in my family spoke of Erasmo and Giuseppe unless prodded, and never comfortably. No one seemed to know anything about anarchists.

The summer my husband and I went to my father's hometown of Saviano, we stayed at a hotel in Naples, right on the bay, looking across to Vesuvius. The water in the bay sparkles as though it is electric. No matter what time of day, the boys of Naples dive from the rocks and float on their backs in the sun.

We are there in late June. I get up early in the morning of June 28 I quietly leave the bedroom and in the bathroom, push open the shutters of the window. The moon is still casting its light on Vesuvius in the distance. Far off, I hear the strays of Naples barking. My thoughts are of Amelia, Erasmo, and Giuseppe.

I see Amelia in a darkened bedroom with the door shut. On the other side, family caring for her children. Cousins, aunts, nieces, and nephews try to quiet their own sorrow, listening for any call from Amelia for comfort, but she is beyond comfort, beyond remedy. She lies curled on top of their bed, the one she shared with Erasmo. The only movement she makes is in her hands, as she wrings Erasmo's handkerchief, the one he gave her the night of the snow, the coldest night of the year, December 31, 1917.

The snow that night was horizontal, pelting the windows. The revelers in their best party attire, sipping wine from small green glasses, were beginning to tire of the wait. Word had begun to circulate that Raffaele Schiavina, who was to speak to the group, had been caught outside of town in the storm and could not get through. Trapped now themselves, the amiable group was growing restless, and the wine was running out, still hours before the toast to herald in the new year. Schiavina was to calm the group, to assure them all would be well in spite of the fearful fever sweeping this new land in which they were viewed as aliens. The *Herald* recently reported that an anarchist cult had been found in the midst of New Britain.

Now, here they were celebrating in a new undisclosed location, safe from discovery, they hoped, and away from their own neighborhood where they normally held meetings and listened to lectures. *Cantate per noi*, the crowd begins to call, gesturing toward Erasmo and Amelia. The husband and wife know all the operas. Everyone in their families did. Erasmo and Amelia look at each other, and shrug their shoulders. *Va bene.* They will sing.

Al tuo fato unisco il mio, son tuo sposo, he sings.

E tua son io, she sings.

Dilegua, o notte!

Tramontate, stelle!

Tramontate, selle!

All'alba, vincerò!

Vincerò! Vincerò! Erasmo sings.

Aria after aria, they sing. Outside, the storm rages. Raffaele Schiavina never arrives.

When the applause begins to fade and the shouts of "bravo" wane, Erasmo takes Amelia's hand, and they venture out onto the covered balcony.

At that moment, the snow stops. Fast-moving clouds reveal a thin path of clear sky. Perhaps, for a second only, a star shines on them before retreating behind advancing clouds. "Who knows when we will be this happy again," Erasmo whispers in her ear. He covers her shoulders with his coat, and they return to the revelry inside. Glasses and voices raised. Her shining body pressed to him. The lovers are enveloped in the clamor of the new year.

But tonight, the night of his death, she is in despair. From time to time, she mumbles imprecations against the land that is taking her life from her, her breath, her heart, her soul. She curses the lawyers, the judge, the jury. She calls on special powers, granted to her by the enormity of her affliction, and casts a most malignant curse on His Excellency, the Honorable Governor Holcomb: *maledizione.*

Not far away, in his cell, Erasmo is in a stupor. He is rocking back and forth. He cannot be relieved of the image in his head, Amelia's last kiss. His sons holding onto her as she stumbles, nearly dropping his infant son. His family being led away. "I lose my brain, I lose my brain," Erasmo repeats as he rocks. The hours pass. There will be no midnight reprieve.

Erasmo is led up the scaffold to the noose.

He is wearing a brown suit and a striped shirt with a white collar and a black bow tie. He is offered the crucifix as the black hood lowers over his head. He pushes the cross away with both his tethered hands. He pays no attention to the priests praying on either side. His tie is removed. His collar is loosened. The rope is adjusted around his neck. Erasmo feels a sudden pull. He is released into the air. He soars. Then, with a crack like thunder, he flies away home.

Giuseppe, praying with the priests and kissing the cross, follows.

In Naples, it is dawn. I hear the low, mournful tolling of bells somewhere in the distance, six in all. Whitman's words come to me in this foreign land that is my ancestral home.

What the study could not teach—what the preaching could not accomplish is accomplish'd, is it not?

. . . .

Suspend here and everywhere, eternal float of solution!

The mystery remains suspended. Ancestors who came before us keep their secrets permanently planted within us. "Be at peace, be at peace," I pray. Great or small, we furnish our parts toward eternity; we furnish our parts. ❦

1-800-555-MARY
BETH GIBBS

I picked up my cell phone to call Charlaine and right outside my window, there it was: smiling pink lips, pale-blue eyes and slim, white hands folded in prayer. Above a golden halo was the words "Virgin Mary Speaks to America Today." Underneath the hands was a telephone number with the instruction, "Call 1-800-555-MARY." I stopped dead in my tracks and laughed before I got mad. I spent at least ten minutes with my hands on my hips and my eyes all squinty, trying to figure out what that billboard was doing in my neighborhood. I was used to the ones that sold Kool cigarettes and Boone's Farm wine, and I wondered how much Madison Avenue planned to charge for salvation.

She looked like the models on those other billboards: size 10, thin, pretty in a washed-out, Eurocentric kind of way. I snorted. What a loony tunes world! The Black Madonna is front and center in many Polish churches, and here is a white Madonna on top of the Nation of Islam's mattress factory. Go figure!

Maybe I wouldn't have been so irreverent if she looked more like the women I knew, but that blonde hair and those blue eyes were a bit much to swallow in a neighborhood where most folks ranged from *café au lait* brown to pitch purple-black with soft, dark eyes and lots of too, too solid flesh.

"Too, too solid flesh." That's Shakespeare. It's from *Hamlet*. I always liked it because I've been trying to melt my too, too solid flesh for too, too, too many years.

I was 250 pounds and counting when Oprah Winfrey went through her weight thing. She got into those size 10 jeans, strutted on stage, and I gave it up for her. "You go, girl!" I screamed. "You go for all of us!" Then she had to drop the size 10 when she ballooned back into sizes 16 and 18. I was crushed. Finally, she hired a personal chef and a trainer, and found a happy medium. I was happy for her, but I couldn't afford a personal chef or a trainer, so I called 1-800-94-JENNY. I tried Nutrisystem, Weight Watchers, and Overeaters Anonymous. I did the grapefruit plan, the protein plan, and the low-fat plan. I sweat to the oldies, took pills, and even paid a three-month visit to Mama Rue's fat farm in the Caribbean. For a New York minute, I thought about having my stomach stapled. But I dumped that idea and gave up trying.

The breakdown did me in. I sat around the apartment watching TV and talking to Charlaine whenever I could get a word in edgewise around her advice about what I should be doing with my life. Charlaine is my best friend, you see, and we used to talk on the phone during *The Oprah Winfrey Show*, swapping opinions about her diets, hair, clothes, and guests. Delores and Charlaine: two sister friends passing the time.

The last time had we talked, I could tell she was all kinds of upset with me.

"Dee," she said, "you have got to pull yourself together. I'm all outa advice. I don't know how else to help you." She sighed.

"And you know I want to. We've been ride-or-die friends since the third grade and if you can't dig yourself out of this hole, you leave me no choice but to figure out how to hold an intervention on your behind!"

The breakdown? Oh yeah, that. Well, I went off one day in the cafeteria at work. I cussed, shook, and howled something awful. Next thing you know, I'm in a straight jacket at the local loony bin, popping Valium like aspirin. The shrink they sent me to didn't have a clue so, as soon as I stopped raving and sank into depression, they gave me a prescription for antidepressants and let me go.

They didn't know what was wrong. I did. I felt unloved. Sure, Charlaine and my family loved me, but their love was the safe love that families and friends are supposed to have for one another. I was missing that bone-deep, accepting love: the kind that wraps around your life and bursts your heart. And it wasn't about men. Many had declared their love for my soft eyes, my ample curves, my southern fried chicken and sweet potato pie. I felt their arms and heard their words, but I never believed they were really meant for me.

Anyways, my depression and I holed up in my apartment. When I needed to talk, I called Charlaine. When I needed food, I called Stop & Shop.

My job had given me a six-week medical leave to get myself together and go back to work. With three weeks to go, I was nowhere near ready and really bummed out. Giving up my job as a systems analyst and not working at all was scary, but going back to work and facing everybody made my insides quake. I knew I couldn't make it on welfare. Too humiliating. I felt like Mount St. Helens before her big bang.

The Mary billboard was just another irritant. And that irritant started to watch me. Her eyes followed me around my living room. They reproached me when I ate, pleaded soulfully with me when I watched TV, and got a hopeful glint in them when I talked to Charlaine. I could feel those eyes glued on me like white on rice. The feeling persisted even when I pulled down the shade.

So that's how it was the morning I woke up with three weeks to go before my day of reckoning. I heaved myself out of bed and waddled past the window to pick up the remote control. I was going to watch the *Today* show and try to ignore Mary like I usually did, but that morning something pulled my eyes to the window and glued them square on the billboard. My jaw dropped. Her eyes had changed color. Now they were brown: a soft, warm, sparkling brown. I shook my head and looked again. No mistake. *Strange*, I thought. *Why would they come back and just change the color of her eyes?* The next day, her blonde hair turned dark brown and started to curl. After that, her skin darkened, her nose broadened, her lips widened, her hair kinked up, and she started gaining weight. I sat by the window night after night trying to catch the midnight painter, but in spite of NoDoz and extra coffee, I never saw a soul. Yet each morning, Mary looked more and more like a fat Black Madonna with a 'fro. Her mouth still wore that lush, glowing smile, and her eyes continued to haunt me.

Many times during those days, I felt an urge to pick up the phone and make the call. Many times my hand reached out, and many times I snatched it back. I knew the billboard didn't make any sense from a rational standpoint, and I am basically a rational, intelligent person. Except for my breakdown, I tend to carefully plan my idiocies. I knew I wasn't hallucinating be-cause I had flushed all the drugs from the hospital down the toilet. Reality was bad enough without drugs. I was depressed and dysfunctional—not stupid.

Finally, when I couldn't stand it a minute longer, I pulled my hand out of a bag of double chocolate macadamia nut cookies, pushed the bottle of Diet Coke aside, grabbed my phone, and punched in the numbers: 1-800-555-MARY.

I heard it ring on the other end and I started to sweat. It rang again and I began to panic. It rang a third time, and I was about to hang up when someone picked up and a voice filled with enough warmth to melt frozen butter in a nanosecond said, "Hello-o-o."

"Uh, hi. Uh, can I speak to Mary please?"

"Oh sure, honey. Is this Delores?"

"Uh . . . uh . . . uh, yeah, this is me," I said as I peered around my apartment. "Listen, am I on *Candid Camera*?"

The voice chuckled. "No, sugar. This is for real. Hang on a minute, will you? She's just getting off the other line."

The other line? Why, I wondered, did this feel like a call to the Psychic Friends Network? I looked around for Dionne Warwick.

"Listen dear, you *will* hang on, won't you?"

Well, really, what did I have to lose? "Yeah, I'll wait," I managed to croak.

There was something disturbingly familiar about Mary's voice when it came on the line. In a way it was like listening to the women in my family. The cadence, pitch, tone, and accent were right on the mark, yet it was different somehow. I couldn't place it and it unsettled me.

"Delores, what took you so long? I've been waiting and waiting to hear from you."

"You have?" My eyebrows shot up to meet my hairline.

"Yes. We've been trying to get through to you for weeks."

"Really?" I put my free hand on my hip, popped it out, and sucked on my teeth.

"Yes! We tried reaching you through your family and Charlaine. You weren't listening. You know, Delores, you're running out of time. We had to resort to something dramatic."

I rolled my eyes. "Uh-huh, and you thought a billboard of the Virgin Mary would be just the thing to get my attention?"

"Well, we send out the word as best we can, but it doesn't always get through the way we intend it. The veil between us is very thin, dear, but it can cloud up."

I sighed. What kind of scam was this woman running?

"The billboard designer and Father O'Leary didn't get the image right. We had to alter it to make our point. I hope it didn't upset you too much."

It didn't compute. Maybe I was having some kind of post-drug hallucination. Discomfort and confusion coalesced and turned into a nasty hunch. I felt it form. The hair on the back of my neck stood up. My head felt poufed like cotton candy. Suddenly, I knew why the voice was so familiar. It was woo-woo time.

"Your name is not really Mary, is it?" I whispered.

"No." She said softly.

"Who the hell are you?" I rasped.

"I think you know."

"Maybe, but I want to hear you say it."

"My name is Delores and I love you."

The weight of those words knocked me off my feet and sat me down on the couch. I was talking to myself! I was talking to the part of me that had never given up; the part I ignored and shunted aside; the part that knew the truth about my inability to feel love, about my feelings of insecurity, vulnerability, and pain; the part that sent me off the deep end, hoping I'd find a way to climb back.

"Delores?"

I sniffled. "Yes."

"Are you still listening?"

I gulped. "Yes."

"Can you love me back?"

"It's hard," I gasped. "I…I don't know how."

"Too hard to love yourself? Oh dear, maybe I'm too late after all. Should I hang up?"

"Nooooooo!" I screamed into the phone. "Noooooo! Nooooooo!"

"Way to go, dear. I think you need a little more time. How about two weeks?"

Two weeks later I went back to work and rejoined the human race. I recycled the Diet Coke bottles, started drinking lemon water and added fruits and vegetables to my Stop & Shop deliveries. Delores-Mother-Mary-Me was right. I'm working on loving myself as I am: big, black, and bodacious. It's slow going but I'm making progress, and I'm still giving it up for Oprah. If she knew about my struggle, I know she'd give it right back and scream, "You go, Delores! You go for all of us!" ◖

CHILDREN OF LIR
NICHOLE GLEISNER

Quiet Sunday.
Innards of October sunshine
coagulate within the trees' amber leaves as
we cross the Housatonic, weaving
in and out of dregs of light.
Feeble stands of young maples cluster together,
their budding branches hungrily browsed
by an ever-increasing population of
whitetail. The numbers that justify
the hunt. Occasional gashes
of blue beyond and above.
Approaching Newtown,
the Pootatuck alongside, clots
of white bobbing in the water,
slowing, perhaps they are singing,
swans, so many of them,
five times over those victims of
Aoife, malicious queen, mean

stepmother. I know that in the first
telling of this tale their human voices
were left within the bone-white bodies
encased in feathers, slender necks bent
by the burden of language.
Yet when I open my window to behold
them now: the utter silence, a castigation. ◆

A WEDDING
SUSAN CINOMAN

I saw pictures of my children on their father's wedding day.
And I wasn't even dead.
It broke my heart to watch them smiling,
holding on to the arm of the lovely bride,
by her side,
their pale skin blending in with her white gown.
And flowers all around.
Their father, looking happier than life, than sun,
than any minute that he met me,
it was easy for him to forget me.
What little girl should have to look at her father
and his beautiful bride and wonder
how their mother, now graying and thick in the middle,
must have looked once by his side?
My time didn't have to go like that,
I pushed it away like a dish I couldn't eat,
made my stomach weak.
I couldn't do it,

I could pursue it, but when it came down to it, couldn't do it.
Cherubs sweet, they gave it their all, those girls,
smiles were real, thank-yous and pleases and pearls,
trying hard to feel what he wanted them to feel.
It became as real
as roses and ribbons that flew through the air.
Light and pretty and better promises made.
That day, my daughters were in the vibrant sun
in the garden, in their stepmother's changing room, in the
trees' shade.
Though I wasn't there, so much of that wedding day, I made. ♦

RENDEZVOUS
CHARLES V. BELSON

The Friday morning after Thanksgiving, I meet my girlfriend at the Plaza Hotel in Manhattan. She's a runaway like me.

I bring my overnight bag. She brings hers. I'm a sophomore at Yale in the first graduating class to admit women. And she's a freshman at Vassar in the first graduating class to admit men.

I met her two months ago at a Vassar mixer. She danced like a pro. I found her attractive and a gifted storyteller. She read Latin and Greek. By the end of the mixer, I knew her SAT verbal scores. They were higher than mine. I also learned that back home in Shaker Heights, Ohio, she got paid to be a go-go dancer in a cage, dancing at private parties to help raise money for charity. We saw each other the next weekend at Yale. She stayed at the Taft Hotel near campus. We spent more weekends at Yale than at Vassar.

By Thanksgiving, we have private nicknames for each other. She calls me Chamlet. She pronounces it *Shamlet*, so it rhymes with *Hamlet*, her favorite Shakespearean antihero. I call her Freelove, because the name was popular with her

Puritan family, especially back when her sixth great-grandfather wrote "Sinners in the Hands of an Angry God."

At the Plaza, she introduces me to her family from Ohio. We drink "nooners" in her grandparents' ninth-floor suite overlooking Central Park. We all have lunch in an alcove off the Edwardian Room on the first floor. Her aunts and uncles take turns telling stories with an amusing or surprising twist. Her grandparents ask me to tell the last story, right after my girlfriend finishes hers. While others speak, I narrow my list of potential stories to these three: "The Roommate," "The Summer Vacation," and "The Runaway."

"The Roommate" focuses on my roommate from Oberlin, Ohio. Every Sunday at exactly 2:00 p.m., his parents call the black rotary phone sitting on the mantel of the fireplace in the living room of our two-bedroom, four-person suite. He makes sure he is always there at 2:00 p.m. to answer. He doesn't want his parents to know that he lives off campus in his girlfriend's apartment. On Saturday nights in October and November, my Vassar girlfriend slept over in the bunk above mine, in the bed my Ohio roommate never occupied. My girlfriend liked this arrangement much better than staying at the Taft Hotel. I did, too.

"The Summer Vacation" story started in June. I worked as a construction cost estimator for a member of the Long Island Builders Institute. When the job ended in August, another one of my three roommates drove to Long Island to pick me up. We picked up our roommate in Ohio on the way to Chicago. We stayed with a classmate who was a community activist for the summer. His side job was helping to organize the antiwar protests at the Democratic National Convention. We arrived the day the protests began, just before dusk. Helicopter spotlights targeted us from above Michigan Avenue. The pilots fired tear gas canisters as we stood in the crowds below. Some couldn't breathe and they dropped to the ground. At ground level, the gas was less dense. They could breathe again. Others ran. They tripped over fallen friends. In Grant Park, thousands of us chanted, "The whole world is watching! The whole world is watching!" Television cameras captured our community activist classmate being bloodied by the nightstick of a Chicago policeman. The news cameras stopped rolling at 9:00 p.m. The protest abruptly ended. TV networks edited their footage in time for the national nightly news. By 10:00 p.m., we were back in our classmate's apartment watching coverage of the protest. We shared a few beers and a few joints. On television, our community activist's bloody head wound looked much more serious than it was. He was glad he looked bad. The whole world was watching.

My third story, "The Runaway," is about me leaving home when I was a child. The story is very dark. Sometimes I heard it retold by relatives at parties. Their version was more like a comedy than the tragedy I remembered. Either way, it was a good story to tell.

As I wait my turn, I listen to my girlfriend tell her parable about the prodigal daughter. When she is four years old, the ice cream man stops his truck in front of her house. She asks her mother to buy a Fudgsicle for her. Her mother says no because it's too close to dinnertime. My girlfriend goes up to her room. She starts packing her overnight bag. Since she can't have a Fudgsicle, she decides to leave Shaker Heights and run away to New York. She loves her Kay Thompson books about the girl named Eloise who lives with her family in the penthouse of the Plaza Hotel. Eloise gets anything she wants, whenever she wants it. My girlfriend grabs her packed overnight bag and runs away to the Plaza Hotel in New York.

She doesn't get far. She circles the block around her house. She can't cross the street because her parents taught her not to cross by herself. A neighbor spots her standing on the corner with her overnight bag. The neighbor calls my girlfriend's mother. Her mother then picks her up at the neighbor's house. My girlfriend is made to unpack her bag, hang everything up, and put everything away, as if nothing happened. But something does happen. Her mother buys her a Fudgsicle the next day when the ice cream man returns and her mother promises to take her on a trip to the Plaza Hotel on her tenth birthday.

After my girlfriend's story, her grandparents politely clap. Their granddaughter gets up from the table. She walks over and gives both grandparents a big hug. She thanks them for helping make possible all nine of her trips to the Plaza. Then she asks me to tell my story. After the Plaza staff serves all of us a light dessert of lemon squares, I decide to tell the dark version of "The Runaway."

Grown-ups say I went missing and I am a runaway, but that's not what happened. I spent most of the day directly across the street from my house. I was playing, running, jumping and splashing, with dozens of kids in the big wading pool in the small park on 164th Street in Queens. No one told me or my parents that before there was a park, dozens of kids were buried in unmarked graves—mostly sick kids, poor kids, and lost and missing kids—as I run, jump, and splash over their unmarked graves.

My mom puts me to bed early. She tells me that my sisters will be my babysitters for two hours. She and my dad will be visiting my aunt and uncle six blocks away. With my eyes closed, I nod my head. Yes, I understand.

My sisters watch the *Ed Sullivan Show*. My mother and

father return home after two hours. My sisters say everything
is fine. My mother heads to my bedroom. My father goes to
the kitchen. My mother shouts, "Our baby's gone!" My father
runs to my bedroom. They don't panic. My sisters help them
search the house, the yard, and the pool. They don't find me.

My father is an FDNY first responder. The kitchen becomes his command post. When he walks into the kitchen, it
looks like the scene of a break-in, or worse. Maybe a kidnap-
ping. The kitchen door to the outside is open. The kitchen table is askew. The chair by the open door is knocked over. But
my father tells my mother that this is no break-in. It's a break-
out. My father calls the NYPD to report that I have run away.
He is more sad than mad. He knows from FDNY experience
there's a chance he may never see me again. At least not alive.

I remember waking up and wanting to be with my mother
and father at my aunt's house. In early summer, it's still light
at eight o'clock at night. To get to my aunt's house, I need to
cross a busy street with a traffic light. I worry about what to
do without a grown-up to help me cross. The light changes
twice. A pretty lady says, "I can help you cross the street." We
cross the street hand in hand, just like I do with my mother.
The lady asks, "How about an ice cream?" I say, "Okay." She
takes me into a pub. Her husband is the owner. She sits me
down on top of the bar. A waitress asks if I would like ice cream.
I say, "Any flavor is fine." My mother taught me to say that.
My mother thinks kids who ask, "What flavors do you have?"
sound like spoiled brats. The pub owner's wife melts when she
hears my response. She says to her husband, "This one is so
polite." Then with a big smile, she winks at her husband and
says, "Finders keepers, losers weepers."

At that moment, I didn't know the pub owner and his wife
had no children. I didn't know his wife wanted to keep me. I
didn't know the pub owner had difficulty convincing his wife

that they should call the police. I didn't know that the police would take me to the New York Foundling hospital at Third Avenue and East Sixty-ninth Street in Manhattan. I didn't know that within minutes of being admitted to the Foundling, examined for signs of abuse, and then released, I would be smothered with hugs and kisses by my mother and father.

It's the kind of day a four-year-old like me has no trouble remembering.

My girlfriend's grandfather stands up. He toasts both of us for our stories about the four-year-old runaways who eventually find each other. After lunch, her grandparents speak with us for a few moments. Her grandmother graduated from Vassar. Her grandfather from Yale. Her grandmother asks her if the Taft Hotel is still open. Her granddaughter says, "Yes, it's still nice, and I've stayed there too." Her grandmother smiles in approval, then quickly changes the subject.

Later, we go for a horse and carriage ride in Central Park with my girlfriend's parents. Her father boasts about his frugality and all the money he saves by having his only child mow the lawn, wash the cars, and clean the roof gutters. I'm the only one who notices that he seriously undertips the carriage driver, so I give the driver a few extra bucks when nobody's looking. My girlfriend's parents go back to the hotel to nap. We walk to the art galleries on West Fifty-Seventh Street. One gallery shows the work of my art professor. He paints still-life oil paintings from memory, without looking at props or photos. Each painting is like a memoir without words.

We freshen up back at the hotel. We meet with her family for cocktails at 6:00 p.m. in her grandparents suite. Then, her family goes to a Broadway show and we go dancing. Her uncle hands me some unexpected extra cash as we leave. I thank him for being so generous. My girlfriend says he's more like an older brother than an uncle.

Tina Turner's thirtieth birthday concert and dance party at the Electric Circus sells out. Flush with unexpected funds, we buy two scalped tickets. Tina Turner sings and dances nonstop. At the end of the concert, she has multiple encores. In her finale, Tina invites women who love to dance to come join her. She performs "Shake a Tail Feather." My girlfriend and the other women who volunteer have the unrestrained energy of caged dancers set free. As my girlfriend dances, I can't take my eyes off her. I tell her she has never danced better.

"Funny you should say that," she says. "When you went to the restroom, a choreographer asked me to audition for the touring version of his Broadway show. The show is *Hair*. It's a hit. He gave me his card. I didn't say no." My girlfriend might be serious about running away to join a traveling show.

The late-night elevator man at the Plaza Hotel takes us from the lobby up to the ninth floor. My girlfriend and I exit the elevator. We walk down the empty corridor to our separate rooms. We've been together for two months. Our rendezvous at the Plaza is winding down. Most runaways never find the people or places they search for, but we're not most runaways. ⬧

SAWDUST
CLAUDIA MCGHEE

Sunday, summer, second day of men's loud voices upstairs
with scraping, banging, wood thudding overhead, the metal
saw blade screeches, shrieks, then silence. They say they
are raising
the roof, building a *dormer,* new bedrooms up there for her
and one brother, a new bathroom, new office for Daddy.

Sawdust settles everywhere, covers everything in sweet-
smelling slippery sharp bits of wood. When they say
"It's time,"
that she's allowed to go look, she tries to scoot now, Daddy
grabs her shoulders, grips hard, shakes her a little,
"Stay away
from the edge!" "Okay okay!" and she squirms away, races

to the stairs, flings open the door, clambers up
hands and feet,
gets halfway and one foot slips on sawdust. She falls
and slides
facedown, bangs her chin on a step then another,
bumps cheek
belly chest, thumps both knees hard before she can
slow herself,
before she can stop her tumble, keep herself from screaming.

Daddy lifts her up, squats in front of her, opens her mouth,
checks for chipped teeth, presses cheekbones, nose, sore chin,
runs his hands
down past collarbones, brief pause on her flat chest,
sighs "I hope
nothing permanent . . . time will tell." She looks at
him, her sobs
stop in one breath. "Nothing broken," he says, but she
feels doomed

somehow, damaged, even though she hurts only a little.
He gives her a slight push, "Go on, but go slower this time!"
She holds the handrail, then stands at the top,
afraid to move.
The entire back wall of the house is gone. All she can see
are a few sticks holding up the roof, letting in the sky. ◆

HOLD THE SUN
MAURA FAULISE

Dusk, from a window I watch
our son, twenty-four, in the backyard
on his knees.
In a dusty tee and Carhartt cap,
he puzzles together
a stone patio, angles the flagstones
and taps each down with a mallet
so nothing shifts.
Silver stone dust rises, surrounds him
as Neil Young warbles a rusty falsetto
from a speaker on the stair:
Every junkie's like a setting sun.

At seventeen he was lost
in the veins
of New England's small towns,
sunk in couches of strangers, vanished
into cars and bars and beds
of otherworldy people
who chased the dragon too.

Star-studded student, muscled
high school crew boat boy gone rogue
into bones, picked-off eyebrows, gray
flesh, just barely alive
in the skin of addiction:
straight fentanyl three times a day.
He should be dead.

Where is my son? so many times gripping
my husband's collar, *Where is my son?*

When he did come around
we were ready: Narcan pens in our pockets
and purses, drawers, gloveboxes,
in the basement beside his old bins
of Legos.
Inject through his clothes, we were told.
There won't be time.

We learned to listen
for the death rattle, the throat-gurgling
that signals overdose.
But how lucky we were, never needed
the needles, never needed
to keep him breathing
while we waited for the ambulance
as he did one night
in the grass, hovering over
his girlfriend's body, pushing
air into her lungs
with his mouth, *please please please please please
don't die,*
his tears spilling
through her teeth.

In these last shards
of sunlight
as Neil young repeats
his dark prophecy,
I want to smash that speaker.
This sun won't set.

Yet I am afraid of statistics, terrified
of time's quick tick. What if
we lose him
after just getting him back?

Our son gathers his tools
in the pink dust,
and I want to
Halt. Time.
With my own two hands
hold that sun up, look
longer at this boy turned man,
here now
working so hard
to set things
right. ◆

DEAD LETTER
JASON WILKINS

I must have been up very late the night before, since when the hammering began at my door, it startled me into the mid-morning, and I signed for the certified letter in a daze. Inside the businesslike manila envelope was my death certificate.

That woke me up.

"Does the certificate have your correct name, address, and Social Security number?" growled the man on the phone when I called to inquire. It did. "Then what are you complaining about?"

"Well, I'm not dead. "

"Give it time," he snarled. He hung up.

I took the bus to work as usual. When I got there, the receptionist in the lobby gave me a scandalized look. "You're late," she said.

"I know," I sighed, "ninety minutes. But you wouldn't believe—"

"That's not what I meant."

When I got to our floor, the desks were all abandoned.

Everyone had gathered in the conference room. The boss was giving a somber speech: "In light of this sad event, I think it best if we close the office for the rest of the—"

He saw me standing at the back of the room. "Oh!" he said, more in disappointment than shock. Everyone turned. I heard a few deflated sighs. "Well," the boss said, "never mind, then. Everyone back to work."

My colleagues ignored me the rest of the morning. "Only that moron could wreck our day off even when he's dead," somebody muttered.

I decided to use my lunch hour to clear up this confusion. The orderly at the morgue looked at me and the death certificate and said, "Everything appears to be in order."

"But I'm not dead!"

"Take it from a professional—you can't fight city hall."

The orderly led me to a cold room in the basement. The wall was covered with square metal doors. One of the metal doors had a Post-ti stuck on it, bearing my name.

"If I don't see myself in there," I told the orderly, "I'm going to be very upset."

He smirked, yanked the door open, and pulled out the slab. On it lay a full-length mirror. I saw both our faces in it.

"I bet someone's feeling pretty foolish right about now," he said.

Before I could start yelling, someone said, "Is this him?" It was a heavyset woman in a lab coat and plastic goggles, carrying a rotary saw in both hands.

"This is him," the orderly told her. Seeing my confusion, he said: "You **did** sign up to be an organ donor, didn't you?"

I got out of there.

Rather than return to work, I took an early bus back home. Someone had left a newspaper behind. Inside was my obituary, only a few lines long. My brother out West must have written it, since it asked that in lieu of flowers, mourners should send donations directly to his post office box. Never borrow money from family.

The mailbox in the lobby contained one letter for me, in which my student loan lender said that it was aware of my recent change of status and offered to collaborate on a new repayment plan that would enable me to meet my ironclad financial obligations.

As I stepped off the elevator and approached my apartment, I saw my girlfriend. The pack on her back was comically overstuffed. She locked my apartment with the spare key I'd given her, then slid the key under the door.

"Oh!" she gasped. "Did you have to startle me like that? Why do you always have to make a scene?"

"I'm sorry if I scared you," I said, "but I'm not actually dea—"

She cut me off. "I have to go," she said. "Dan's waiting."

I heard a familiar horn bleat in the street. "Dan from your office?" I asked, bewildered. "You let Dan from the office drive your little red Corvette?"

She reached out as if to touch my face, then seemed to think better of it. "Things have been dead for a while."

I went inside to discover that she'd taken all my best DVDs and T-shirts, along with every gift she'd ever given me. But the laptop was still there—she always said it was a piece of crap—so I dully sat down and googled myself. Nothing came up except a message that said "404 Not Found—Why Are You Even Bothering?"

I took a nap. It didn't last long, for my landlady came through with a group of college students. They glared in my direction. "Sorry about the mess," my landlady said. "We'll have the garbage hauled away immediately."

They proceeded to ignore me. I felt a bit like crying but that was when I noticed the cockroach crawling out of the hole in the floor by the radiator. It skittered in place for a moment, then caught sight of me and froze. It's little antennae clicked back and forth. A moment later, a dozen cockroaches filed up out of the hole behind it and they all marched in a line straight at me. I fled.

That was a while ago. I don't know how long ago, exactly—time gets away from a person in a place like this. I know I must have made my way from the apartment to the morgue somehow, and maybe it's a little strange that nobody saw me climb on this slab and slide myself into the wall, but who's to say what's really strange, in the end? In here, I bother no one, and no one bothers me. What more could you want out of life? ◈

AFTER THE PROTEST
WENDY TARRY

(For A.)

> Open your mouth for the mute,
> in the cause of all who are left desolate.
>
> —Proverbs 31:8

If you breached the peace,
it was as a whale breaches
the salty water,
a smack of astonishment
to remind us
there are giants in the deep.
Still,
after the protest,
they listed you in the police blotter
of the small-town paper.
I say cut it out
with kitchen scissors,
tack it to the mudroom wall,

by the braids of garlic,
the drying leeks,
the jars of maple syrup
tapped from your trees.
Let it weather there,
let its edges curl,
let it ripen
with all these things that have known
dark earth
and secret growth.
When you're an old lady
shucking off your garden boots,
look at it,
that little mellowed clipping,
and say
"I stood, I cared,
I bothered
even if they bothered me right back."
And that paper,
yellow as wild honey,
might hold a trace of sweetness yet. ◑

AFTER THE PARTY
MEGHAN EVANS

Sometimes you think you've won. Sometimes you stand in the middle of a crowd and think you really know your way around the world, and best of all, you know yourself. And you believe you've got everyone else figured out. They're puppets in your hand.

Then the crowd parts and you find yourself standing at the top of a rail, looking down at the concrete pool below, and you realize, kid, you ain't shit.

You're the guy who stayed back in the second grade; who got caught every time he sneaked out of the house; the guy who, to impress some girls, lied and said he could pull off an ollie nose grind into the pool's vert ramp, sure, no problem. You're the guy for whose death the school will set up trauma counseling, because, dude, you're going to die.

You look back at the crowd. Honestly, you suddenly think, who cares if those girls are hot? Can't you walk away from this? There must be other, better girls. But everyone is chanting your name, which no one knew ten minutes ago, and you've been trying to make friends for weeks in this new town with no luck. So kid, it's looking like you've got little choice.

You have two comforts. One, if you are stupid enough to go through with this, you deserve to die, and two, a freak skateboarding accident where your head juices against the concrete walls of the pool is no pansy death. No one will say later that you were crazy for not just walking away. It'd be rude to your memory.

You had no intention of throwing in the life towel tonight. Sure, Connecticut is freezing and no one wants to be friends with the new kid when he shows up in January and doesn't know what "that's brick" means, but things aren't so bad. They aren't "comforted by the prospect of death" bad. You just wanted to meet some nonjerks, have fun, stop missing your friends back home, stop calling New Mexico home.

You overheard people talking about the party during math and decided to go. The house wasn't far from your new place, a couple blocks, so you grabbed your skateboard and rode down. You almost killed yourself on a patch of black ice. It was camouflaged in the dark. No one warned you about the invisibility of ice.

Inside the warm house people cliqued together. You said hi to a few who smiled but wouldn't talk. This, you thought, standing there trying to look at ease, is exactly how you felt that summer in France when all you could understand was "hello" and "no skateboarding allowed." Your mom, a professor, was doing research, and you, thirteen, tagged along, thinking a trip abroad would be cool, that Spanish and French were close enough, that if you wanted to, you could reinvent yourself. Instead you spent the summer learning loneliness.

You tried to explain to other kids that you liked hanging out in the park, too, and all types of music, *la música, la musique,* but, though the kids smiled and shook your hand, they never tried to get to know you, because, well, they already had *amigos*, *les amis*, and who wants to spend their summer dragging around some Mexican American kid who can't communicate? Communicating felt interchangeable then with relating.

So now, in Connecticut, you think, this should be a piece of cake. You all speak the same language, at least. You're a nice guy, fun. Your parents raised you *un caballero*. You didn't think you'd succumb to peer pressure.

Looking down at the empty pool you realize that your street in Hartford, la rue de Paris, and even your grandparents' calle en la Ciudad de México, really aren't that different, though everyone swears they are, and then, well, it makes you happy at first, that the world feels so universal, you know, as a dying thought. But then it makes you sad that everywhere things feel the same, yet no one wants to embrace similarities. You could be a thousand places in the world right now and the buildings would all be walls and windows, the people looking out joyful or miserable.

You drank a few beers contemplating that invisible something that holds everyone together or apart. It was hard enough to be new in town without also standing alone at a party, everyone noticing you by yourself but not coming up to say hey. You gathered all your calm nerves and hung on to them like balloon strings. As best as you could, you floated over to this group of girls who were all smiling, and that seemed friendly enough.

You said something like, "Smoking, huh?" *Pendejo*.

Two giggled, one stared, the other said, "Want to share?"

She had the joint between her fingers and held it out. You'd never smoked but understood the concept so took it, pressed it against your lips. It was damp, lipstick smudged the end pink. You didn't cough, like so many people in the movies, and so congratulated yourself on a small accomplishment. The talker said, "What's your name?"

"Gael. I just moved here."

"Obviously." They chirped and rolled their eyes.

They all stood with their weight on one foot and moved their hands when they spoke and looked stunning. You couldn't follow everything they said, they were gossiping and you didn't know David or Alizé.

When the conversation fizzled, probably because you were there, awkwardly listening, they turned their interest on you. You spilled all the details. Albuquerque, seventeen, only child, January, skateboarding.

"Cool! Can you do tricks?" None of the girls introduced themselves, like they'd humor you with interest but only for tonight, unless you impressed them.

You explained all your tricks. They were not impressed.

"Do you know Robin? He skates," one said. She had long black hair. She looked vaguely Peruvian.

"No. Is he here?" Common ground, a friend?

They shrugged. To torque your mystique, you lied. You could do all sorts of tricks, just like the X Games.

Then they got excited. "Show us! Let's go to the pool!"

Grabbing one another's slender hands and yours, they pulled you outside into the February chill. Put there's a pool at this house on the list of things you didn't know.

And now here you are, with a crowd in love with your eminent demise. A list of things you thought you had:

Common sense

A safety buzz

Cojones

You're scared shitless, though, so bravery is off the table as far as bragging rights in the afterlife. Why have so many people come outside? It's cold. Isn't there anything else to do at this party?

Time's up. You just have to do it or be teased and alone

for the rest of high school. For a second you think you can handle solitude, but then, you just kick off toward the rail and try for glory.

Every *z* of your safety buzz is gone, which is probably a positive. You ride the rail and a cheer barks out, but you fumble your feet and miss your board on the landing and smash against the side of the pool.

White and purple lights burst in your eyes. Pain explodes in your arm, but this means you're alive. You're alive.

Mierda. Dios mío. You scrape skin back onto your elbow.

It could've been a lot worse. Yes, everyone is laughing and yes, your elbow is gushing blood, but people seem impressed that you tried.

You call out, "Fucking ice!" and blame it on the invisible. People disperse without haranguing you too much. Or helping you at all.

You walk from the deep to the shallow end, snatching your board and cradling your arm, and this platinum blonde meets you there. She's small, has these huge eyes.

"You did that for attention," she says mildly.

"So?"

"I'm wondering what you'll do for love." She doesn't smile, which weirds you out. Is she hitting on you? She pulls a gauze pad and a thick roll of Ace bandage from an enormous purse. "What's your name?"

"Gael." Did she not hear people chanting it?

"I'm Noelle. Sit down, I'll do you up."

You obey. She Halloween ghosts you in gauze and bandages, her thin fingers light as air. You want to say your names sound similar, that it's astounding, how much each person has in common with the next, but you don't because people aren't sentimental, and when you are, they just think you're crazy. Different is as scary as ghosts.

When she's got your arm tight in its little winding sheet, she says, "Why did you want that attention?"

"Friendship." You're surprised it isn't obvious.

"They won't be your friends."

She is so bizarre. She doesn't follow her statement up with any qualifications, about them or you, she just stares. Then she squeezes your arm.

"Ay! *Dios!* Fuck!" You stare at her and don't know what to say.

People have retreated inside. You're not sure if you should go back in or just leave. You don't know whose house this is, or the time, or what you'd do inside. Your dad said, "Be home by midnight." He trusted you, and imagined people would want to hang with you until then.

"You speak Spanish?" Noelle asks.

You nod, wary of her hand. "Do you?"

"French," she says. "Not very well. But someday I'll go to France and become better."

"I've been to Paris," you say.

"Really? Tell me everything!" She grabs your hands and without exerting any pressure pulls you into the house. You tell her everything. She smiles and her huge eyes sparkle. She says she's a senior so maybe she'll go this summer. You say you're a sophomore, making sure to include that you're sixteen, not fifteen, and you'll get your mom's tips for her, too.

Noelle goes to the bathroom and when she returns she says, *c'est étouffant* in the house, giggling, so you divert to the front porch. It isn't too hot inside and it's obvious she's just as uncomfortable in the crowd as you. No one says hi or calls out to her. It makes sense, she's a trip, but you wish it made more sense, because also: she's nice. You almost tell her that the word *invisible* is the same in English and in Spanish and in French, but you don't. At best it's sentimental to say so and at worst it's pathetic, it reveals too much about how you feel in Hartford. You wish you could hurry up and know the score.

She's spread her limbs across the porch steps. She's skinny, like a palm tree, her long arms delicate fronds. She's chattering again about after graduation. The yard is quiet. You start to feel comfortable with her awkwardness.

Then this guy stumbles outside. He's bleeding and you wonder if he tried the pool trick, too, but laughter streams out behind him and tension sucks at the air. No one offers him gauze. He gives the crowd the finger. Noelle whispers, "You have to click with the right clique. Otherwise." Her eyes follow the guy down the street like she knows that lonely walk.

Noelle sounds like a prophet. "In public everyone acts big. But you have to consider *after* the party. Eventually you have to go home and answer your questions." She returns inside, and you follow, watching all these invisible strings tighten and break loose around you, like a bunch of balloons, like water hardening into ice.

The girls see you with Noelle. They crowd, say, "Ew, what are you doing?"

They must be talking to her; you're the lame kid who crashed in the pool, after all—but they're looking at you.

"Talking," you say, unsure how to sound.

"Yeah but why to *her?*" the maybe-Peruvian girl says.

"She's nice." You're off balance worse than you were riding into the pool.

"She's a whore." The girl grabs your arms, pulls you close. "She wants to fuck you and give you herpes."

Noelle is on her feet now, too, but she's silent. These girls are not forgiving. They are more closely related to wild animals than to mothers and aunts. You picture them stalking the deserts of your childhood and it seems completely natural that you'd find them there. Long, ragged hair, sharp tongues, claws out.

"She is nice," you say, but was she hitting on you? Is that bad? Almost everything about her is on the list of things you don't know. And then there's graduation. Noelle would leave you behind in June. You don't want to be alone for the next two years.

"I am nice," Noelle says quietly, her eyes searchlights.

"Yeah, nice to any guy who'll fuck you," the girl with braids says. "Don't pick on our skateboard buddy." She tugs at your arm and you bump against her breasts. When Noelle doesn't leave, she says, "We said back off, you dumb bitch. He's ours. Don't stand near her, Gael." She pulls you a few steps back. She pronounces your name "Gail."

"I'm nice," Noelle whispers, looking directly at you, her light turned off.

The four girls laugh, and it's like a shove against Noelle's chest. You can see clearly it's like that.

She turns and melts away like their cruelty is a blaze. "Ugh," one girl laughs. "Good riddance."

"Hey, come on," you start, much too late.

"Forget her. She's a bitch. You don't know her so you don't know."

She's not a bitch, you know that, but you don't say anything. Click with cliques is also something you know.

The laughing girl says, "Come meet Robin."

Obviously they think that what they've just done is cool. The ladder to the top is hung with bodies. They want to collect you.

With the air the way it is—tight—you can't figure out how to say no. It's tight between walls, tight in your esophagus. Your heart is tight in your chest, the only muscle that's working, because you absolutely let the girls pull you into the kitchen, away from Noelle, to meet this blond guy who looks like a skater, and who seems nice, but how can you know yet? And what does it matter when suddenly you realize: You are not nice? Are you going to let these girls collect you until it pays off? You went into that pool for this chance. In lieu of friendship, will you settle for popularity? In Connecticut maybe you'll have things in common with people, but will you have anything left in common with the person you were before?

You'll see Noelle drag on her coat and rush for the door. You'll see the maybe-Peruvian girl trip her, and she'll crash against her slender knees, and like that guy outside, no one will help her up, including you. She'll have a hard time standing, she'll look so confused and she'll stumble again.

Can you blame it on the invisibility of ice? Can you even really believe that? 🜚

WRITING HOME
AIMEE POZORSKI

While out to lunch with a dear friend recently, I pulled out my battered wallet and insisted I would pay. My friend took one look at the holey thing made of recycled book covers and said something I will not soon forget: "Oh, that wallet! My daughter likes to pretend she is poor, too." There is a lot to unpack here, and not time for everything, but I wanted to focus on the words *pretend* and *poor*. Is that what I was doing, I wondered, carrying that tattered thing around with me in my pocket all those years, "pretending" I was still the poor girl who grew up in the 1980s near Green Bay, Wisconsin, a daughter of uneducated parents? As a tenured, full professor living in New Britain, Connecticut, married to a similarly privileged professional, I have begun to ask myself why I might pretend that I am poor.

My friend was wrong about one thing. Her statement about her daughter seemed to indicate she did not understand how well I loved that tattered wallet. Looking back now, it is a bit sentimental, really, but it was a gift reminding me every day that my husband and I are connected by our love of books.

My friend was also very right about something else. I do still cling to my class background, especially the poverty I didn't realize I grew up in until I moved away. I cling to my scrappy childhood—not through clothing nor eating habits nor a battered wallet, but through the size and age of my current home: a postwar twelve-hundred-square-foot Cape Cod with faded aluminum siding in New Britain, a former factory town that, like Green Bay, has suffered from loss of industry, white flight, and a hideous highway running through downtown. I live there because I love it. I love it because it reminds me of home.

In many ways, my story begins in 1981. When my parents, who managed to survive financially together, divorced and fell apart. I was eight years old and living in a small midwestern town where, excluding football players, the best jobs were in factories making toilet paper, paper towels, diapers, and sanitary pads. Most middle-class people did not have college degrees because they could afford to raise a family with only a high school diploma and a union job at the meatpacking plant or the paper mill. People around me used such phrases as "yeah der hey" (meaning "yes") and "dem dere" (meaning "those").

Even though neither my mother nor father went to college, we were eventually able to live comfortably in a white colonial in a brand-new subdivision, indicating that we had actually made it. But in 1981, in that brand-new home, things began to fray. I am not sure what happened first: the collapse of the economy or the collapse of my parents' marriage. It all runs together. My mother's cousin had just committed suicide, Montgomery Ward was handing out massive layoffs, including my dad, who was a general merchandise manager; and my mother, who had always been very pretty and maybe just a little unsettled, began to come undone. I knew it the minute I saw my mom walk in the house, long past dinner on a weeknight. My father had bought a new, champagne-colored Thunderbird—his dream car, one he could not afford—and had forgotten to pick her up from work. She walked ten miles in wedge heels, over a bridge, with her mascara running. When she walked through the door, the setting sun lit her up from behind as if to say, "everything is about to change."

A few days later, she told my three-year-old sister and me that she was leaving my dad. It was the time, after all, when women were entering the workforce and becoming increasingly independent. Meryl Streep and Dustin Hoffman had recently played out the long drama of divorce in the 1979 hit film *Kramer vs. Kramer*, while my mom would blame my dad for not having any money and my dad would look sad and retreat. My sister celebrated: one house suddenly became two, and she was excited to look for the second. I was much less certain things would turn out okay.

When my parents divorced, my mother, sister, and I moved from the colonial in Green Bay to a small town just outside the city limits called De Pere. Since he was recently laid off and could not pay the mortage he and my mom once shouldered together, he organized a tag sale (*rummage sale*, as we say in Green Bay) and sold the record collection, the antique hutch, the grandfather clock, and the china. All before a sympathetic neighbor called my mom at work to say, "He is getting rid of everything."

Meanwhile, my mother rented, for $285 a month, a very small flat on the dodgy end of town. Sewage occasionally flooded the basement. We received government cheese, ate Dinty Moore beef stew out of a can, and every once in a long while, as a treat, we binged on Little Debbie snack cakes. In order to maintain the facade of middle-class life, my mother enrolled me in a Catholic school she couldn't afford. But she tithed, apparently, and the Notre Dame sisters felt sorry for us. I had special tickets for reduced lunch. I can still taste the boxed chocolate milk I received daily with my green, crumpled tickets. To this day, my name is published in government documents somewhere because my dad owed more in back child support (long since forgiven, by the state at least, when my sister turned eighteen) than any other divorced dad in the state of Wisconsin. In school, I remained an outsider: a Catholic school girl whose parents committed the ultimate sin.

When I was in sixth grade, my mom had what we thought was surely a housing breakthrough, the long-awaited sign that we were moving up for real this time: a two-story house on Lawton Place, the good end of town, with white clapboard and black shutters. It was up for sale for twenty-eight thousand dollars and not worth the land it was set upon. It was a half of a house. This is not a metaphor. In retrospect, it felt to me like Edgar Allan Poe's House of Usher, a house divided in two and cracked down the middle, with the second half relocated a few blocks away. The house was so tilted that when my rich Catholic school friends came over, they pretended to roll down the slope of the house as if we were all in an amusement park.

A family doctor once owned our side of the house. He died and left behind anatomy books in the basement and a rock collection. I never really understood, after moving in, if the rocks represented a solid foundation or a heavy albatross weighing down all of us.

Despite the tilt of the house and its crumbling foundation, my mom often sighed contentedly in those days and said: "Oprah should invite us on her show so our little family of three can share our success story with others." I see it differently. After all, my mom had to sleep with a banker to get a mortgage. I still remember his name: Glen. "Thank God for Glen," my mom once said, long after the Lawton house was bulldozed to make space for someone else's garden. The house number was

807: the same number of the suite in Atlanta's city hall where my husband and I secured our marriage license in 2001.

After that house on Lawton Place, I moved to La Crosse to attend a four-year teaching comprehensive college like the one where I now teach. After that, I enrolled in an MA program in English at Milwaukee's premier Jesuit institution, Marquette University, where I still felt radically misplaced. I was humbled by the Jesuit mission of teaching and service yet daunted by the financial wealth of the Marquette undergraduates and overcome with worry my professors would learn that I didn't belong there as a working-class kid from a small town and the first in my immediate family to attend college.

Never was this tension between the privileged undergraduates and my own limited universe more palpable than in the classroom while reading aloud. I was uncomfortable speaking in public. The idea of reading poetry aloud in a classroom full of upper-crust kids made my throat dry and my tongue tied. "Are your parents deaf?," a psychoanalyst at Emory, where I earned my doctorate, would ask me over dinner many years later. I didn't have an answer for the analyst at the time.

Fifteen years later, I finally have a response: my parents were not deaf, just poor and uneducated. It is as though I am afraid of speaking too loudly, of speaking up, of using my million-dollar vocabulary unwittingly to shame my family in their unknowing. As a child of a working-class family, I have learned to practice caution when writing home, so as not to stray too far from my roots. Our families encourage us to leave the small towns we were raised in order to see the world. But to return to that small town too smart, too rich, too educated, too knowing is, in itself, an insult and familial betrayal. I must always remember my place. That is our paradox.

After all, I do remember my place. I was born in a flat in a three-story house on Polish Hill in Manitowoc, Wisconsin. All children of immigrant families from Polish Hill carry in their bones the original structure of these homes: the elderly Polish owners lived on the ground floor and looked after their younger Polish renters, stacked one on top of another, each struggling in their own way and dreaming of one day getting out.

I, in theory, got out. I now live in New Britain, a Polish town I love. Our house, the one where we have raised our son, is aluminum sided, white with red shutters, twelve hundred square feet, two bedrooms, and a bath and a half. It is not the kind of luxury home my ancestors dreamed about when crossing the Atlantic in search of a better life. When contractors looking for work come by and say the look of the house is outdated, I roll my eyes, say okay, and close the door. My husband and son talk about moving to a bigger, newer home to reflect our upward mobility. They are excited about the possibilities. Yet, when I run my fingers over my tattered wallet, I start to worry. Parents get divorced when they live in a nice house. I find comfort, not in the promise of a new home, but in pretending I am poor. It means I am a loyal daughter. It means that, although I have made it, I haven't strayed too far. ♦

HONORING HER LIGHT
KIRAN MASROOR

my grandmother stayed up with me once.
in her flickering kitchen, we sat and peeled
the skin off orange mangoes,
ripeness lingered as humidity does.

and the bits of red skin stayed under my
fingernails even when she tried to scrub them off.
time made origami of her skin, her palms were
wrinkled paper cranes, and the mangoes would not go.

dawn waits giddy eyed outside the window.
the mosquitoes swarm deliriously in the mango air
puffing out of our house, enough sweetness
to make the trees swelter and hunch over.

the sun peeks out, set clean against the blood-
peach pit of the sky. when I notice her sunspots,
I am happy they are that: dark spots of sun
against the pale watercolor of skin.

maybe she touches my cheekbone with her
softened hands, her fingers like gentle architecture.
maybe she bends her spine like the trees, to look
in my eyes for the parts of her that life tore away.

maybe there are no maladies as sweet as
dreaming of her, of her mango perfume.

my grandmother rests on the hind limbs of the earth,
will blur into the wind when she is finally set loose,
will run as far as she can go, the earth spinning below
her feet as she dances, the way she does. ✦

CUTTING MY HEART OUT WITH A BUTTER KNIFE
SARAH DARER LITTMAN

Losing Dad to Alzheimer's
is like having my heart cut out with a butter knife.
The hurt is dull, slow, and constant.
Sometimes, the knife hits a nerve;
the pain becomes a raging flood
pouring into an abyss.

Like the time Mom and I visit and
there is a handbag on the chair in Dad's room—
one that doesn't belong to my mother.
I look at the bag, and then at her,
worrying about how she's feeling.
I know it probably belongs to the lady
in the room next door
who kissed Dad on the mouth in front of my mother,
and me,
and my kids.

That day, my daughter was furious
about the transgression.
"How dare she! Grandpa is married to Grandma!"
she fumed, with a teenager's certainty of right and wrong.
I had to explain that sometimes this happens
when you live perpetually in the now
because the disease has robbed your past
and your future.

But today, the kids aren't with us;
it's just Dad, Mom, and me.
I see my mother notices the bag, too,
and we exchange a glance that tells each other everything.
Then Dad sees our faces—really sees them.
He looks from the bag on the chair,
to me, then to my mother, and he has a rare moment
of clarity.
His eyes fill with tears, and he says to Mom and me, "*You're*
my family."
He can't stop crying because he's just realized
that he's cheated on Mom.
He's cheated on *us*, on our family,
and even though he won't remember it a few
hours from now,
in this moment, he does.

And you understand why they call it heartbreak,
because in this room,
at this moment,
everyone's heart is fracturing into a thousand pieces.
But only two of you
will remember it
tomorrow. ♦

TRANSPLANTED
JANET L. BANNISTER

It is the winter of 2009. I wake on Christina's back porch, a temporary refuge now that I've left my husband. I am homeless and nearly friendless. This space with its long row of windows only permits the twin bed, a fit like ribs around lungs. There is an ancient, hulking, out-of-tune piano at the foot of my bed and a hand-me-down dresser wedged in the space between the wall and the headboard. I am the central figure in a Russian nesting doll: inside layers of pain and shame, inside jeans and a sweatshirt and socks, inside a borrowed comforter and cat companions. Under the final layer of skin and a few tattoos is me—the quivering, hollow core. An electric radiator exhales feebly. My breath escapes this sarcophagus in frosty plumes, blurring the only three cards on the wall: *Season's Greetings* from my employer (Stop & Shop), *Happy Holidays* from my attorney, and *Merry Christmas* from Christina.

Reality smacks me as the fog of sleep clears. Wrapped in a blanket, I trudge to the deck where I smoke Pall Malls and watch squirrels spiral up trees. I am a shaking, crying tangle of nerves. The Pall Malls and squirrels help, as does the wine I pour from the spigot on the box of red sometimes before lunch. Every other day when they are not at their dad's, my seven and eight-year-old girls, Chloe and Cassidy, are here with me. I pull myself together for them. Christina has given them the smaller bedroom, reassembling her kids' old bunk beds and letting us paint. A window separates my porch bed from their bunks. At night, we open it and read *Harry Potter* books aloud. Soon, we'll be in our own apartment. Later, I'll kick the cigarettes. For now, I am here, incubating until I can stand on my wobbly, new-life legs. For years, I'll live like a nomad without roots: a one-year lease here, a two-year lease there. Part of me will always live at Christina's.

Christina and I met at a wake back in 2005. My elderly friend, Virginia, had passed unexpectedly. Heart failure during her ladies' guild meeting. I was heartbroken. I'd been introduced to Virginia by a mutual friend and we'd hit it off. I became a regular tea drinker in her ramshackle, hilltop house, jammed full of history. The shelves that lined her walls housed her dolls and shoeboxes full of postcards from pen pals. She'd greet me in her entry with a hug, show me the buds on her Christmas cactus, and loan me books from her library. Virgina's birthday, like mine, was on New Year's Eve, and she'd call me to exchange birthday wishes. She taught me to knit and I'd thread her sewing needles. We would giggle and lament in her little kitchen, eating cucumber and cream cheese sandwiches from blue willow plates. Knowing Virginia taught me that being friends—being soul mates—has nothing to do with age.

When seeing her in the casket, those once-twinkling eyes forever closed, I wept. I made my way through the line of family. I only knew Emma, Virginia's sister, but offered tearful smiles to the others. *I'm sorry for your loss.* One sad-looking woman introduced herself as Christina, Virginia's niece. I told her I was Janet, a friend. We'd heard of each other. *My niece came and painted my door last night. We drank port!* We stood clasping hands, sharing sorrow, and vowed to have coffee. A week later, I knocked on the door of her little house, a homemade blueberry pie in my hand.

Christina bustled me into the kitchen and gestured to the postcards and envelopes fanned out on the table. "I've been getting these every day," she said. "Look! From Australia, Florida, Switzerland!" A teapot hummed on a burner.

"Are these from Virginia's pen pals?"

They were. Christina had written letters, letting friends around the world know Virginia was gone and responses poured in. We talked deep into the night, finding the strange and familiar parts of each other. Soon, our visits were routine. My girls were always eager to accompany me. They took to Christina right away and knew there was always something fun for them at her house: a batch of new kittens, watercolors to paint with, warm apple muffins. Our friendship is old and broken in now, a favorite sweater. We think of each other as an inheritance: each of us something Virginia left for the other.

Four years after our introduction, when my marriage implodes, I sit in my Saturn Astra facing the ball field in a park not far from my marital home. Already, even though my things are still there, crammed into boxes by the basement couch where I've been hunkering in lieu of a better plan—sleeping fitfully and worrying about confrontations—I no longer think of the house as home. I need a destination.

"Do you think," I say into the cell phone, "that the girls and I could stay with you just for a…."

"Yes!" She cuts me off before I can say my spiel about how it won't be for long. "We can clean out Curt's old room for the girls. You can use the porch. I need to clean that out anyway."

I weep with gratitude.

In the days I live at Christina's, I am a Humpty-Dumpty broken mess, crying in between grocery store work shifts and the two classes I'm enrolled in at the nearby community college. My Baptist background isn't making these life changes any easier. Their answers are black and white: a vow is a vow. I spent years feeling oppressed in ways that were hard to define, confiding in women who advised me to pray and to submit. I spent countless mornings, head bowed over my open bible and morning coffee, begging God to help me love this angry, king-of-the-castle guy I could never seem to please. I highlighted bible verses. I clung to them with diminished hope. "A wife of noble character, who can find? She is worth far more than rubies." (Proverbs 31:10). Over time, I unraveled. I cried all the time and tried to fix it with antidepressants. Eventually, it became clear the straight and narrow path was one I couldn't walk, my steps more like the staggering gait of someone failing a roadside sobriety test. I needed connection and acceptance.

With Christina, I found my way out of my prison and landed in her safe, transitional home, but my exit wasn't graceful. I was ostracized by people who thought the answer was as simple as me needing to "get right with God." Yes, the catalyst for change was another man—one I'll eventually regret—but who made my departure possible. Many Bible verses condemn my behavior, but no one saw the tension within my marital home that thickened the air and manifested in a chronic anxiety I now wear like chain mail. When I talk about God being mad or the crushing guilt and judgment I feel, Christina waves a hand and mutters about "prescriptive morality," or rolls her eyes and says, "I don't think Jesus is like that." She reminds me I am no Hester Prynne and we aren't Puritans. Christina grew up Catholic but has come to her own conclusions summing up her philosophy by saying, "I believe everyone is pretty much doing the best they can." Her biggest concern rests with whether I am okay, rather than worrying how sinful I am. With her support, I keep getting up and facing life.

Over the next couple years, many things will change. My divorce will be finalized. I'll have my own little basement apartment up the road where I will lay in bed at night listening to my neighbor's screeching parrots upstairs. I will have worked out a deal with my maxed-out Visa that was my only means of hiring a lawyer and will be paying my way out of debt. I'll be thinking about becoming a nurse's aide. Christina and I will graduate together, both of us getting associate's degrees. The affair that served as an escape hatch from my previous life will have fizzled away, and I'll have found some new friends. Ten years later, I'll have my bachelor's degree and my own little house. But now I am a seedling springing from a sidewalk crack, digging deep and stretching toward the light.

The road leading to Christina's house is a roller-coaster: a narrow, fraying ribbon of blacktop that twists and dips, hugging the rusted guardrail beyond which the land drops away sharply, yielding to the rocky waters of the cove. My car knows the way. There is room to park by the crumbling stone wall edging her tiny, flower-filled yard. Gardens: unruly plantings where something is always happening—bleeding hearts that drip rosy blooms in early spring; perennial bulbs that send up daffodils, tulips, and lilies. Window boxes burst with color. Azaleas nestle up against the siding. Starry-yellow forsythia stretch their gangly arms. At the corner of the house, a rose of Sharon transplanted from her mother's yard. Against the neighbor's chain-link fence, a line of prickly raspberry bushes I steal handfuls from in late summer.

Around the back of the house, the yard slopes steeply down to the cove. Partway down is a crooked pine tree Chloe planted when we lived there and she came home from third grade with a sapling for Arbor Day. The worn path through the meadow-like grass weaves between tall tulip and beech trees and past an inverted wooden boat with peeling blue paint. It seemed to sink into the earth. Down by the water, there is a firepit Christina dug out and ringed with large rocks. All four seasons, we gather here, brushing the spiders and leaves from the motley collection of lawn chairs to light fires for toasting marshmallows or hot dogs. We watch the water, sparkling like diamonds in the sun and reflecting pink and orange sky at day's end. Swans and mallards paddle and dabble. Sometimes we go out in kayaks, paddling under the train bridge and into the Thames. We stay by the fire until late, watching the fireflies and jumping at the sound of deer smashing through the brush.

A stone cat perched on the step by the front door dangles beads at Mardi Gras and a holly wreath in December. The door is perpetually unlocked. We are welcome anytime. Whenever I open the door, a cat darts in or out. It's a small house—two bedrooms, one bath—clearly the home of an artist, a hippie. Original artwork takes up every available bit of wall space—Christina's, her children's, my children's. Books crowd the shelves, many with gold-edged pages and cloth-bound covers. A gas stove hunkers at the center of the house. Over it hangs a mirror in an ornate frame. Forgoing traditional window treatments, Christina has accented her windows with jewel-toned scarves that hang from rods of driftwood. Every surface features candlesticks, frames, plants, and figurines. Things are lovely, quaint, and occasionally creepy, such as her ventriloquist dummy slumped eerily against a one-eyed teddy bear.

Whenever I cross the threshold, memories swirl....How every year on my birthday, we gather for the SYFY Channel's marathon of *The Twilight Zone*, snacking and playing a game of "*Twilight Zone* Bingo" we invented ourselves. How on

Thanksgiving, we listen to Alice's Restaurant and eat stuffing served from a pumpkin shell. How I've become part of a motley crew: Christina's children who come to holidays toting guitars and break into spontaneous performances; her ex-husband with the long silver ponytail and a fondness for crossword puzzles; Ray, the retired submarine captain who always brings a bottle of red; an eclectic mix of friends and family with Christina at the hub. I sometimes gaze around from where I sit, legs tucked under me in a wicker chair, and consider the crowd. We are our own island of misfit toys. A mix of artists and writers and musicians. Deadheads and liberals and rednecks. Intellectual and arthritic. Divorced, widowed, medicated, addicted, renting, working, getting by. Here, I've never felt judged or self-conscious.

Often, it's just Christina and I, burning candles and playing music. Neil Young. Leonard Cohen. The Rolling Stones. Sitting on the deck or at the kitchen table, we tell our secrets and drink our wine. Now, my daughter Cassidy, unexpectedly pregnant and not quite done with her nuclear engineering degree, stays with Christina. Once again, Christina cleaned out a bedroom. Once again, she magically made everything fit, storing things in the basement and letting Cassidy strip off the old wallpaper and paint. In that safe place, Cassidy's belly swelled as she assembled a crib and knit hats. When the time came, baby Landon's first ride home was down that snaking road, to a place where he would come to know cats and Jerry Garcia and Harold and his purple crayon.

I go over and watch little Landon on Mondays. Normally, he is good natured: his easy smiles turning his dimples into deep, adorable pits, laughter bubbling up in response to my antics. Last Monday, however, Christina comes home to find me pacing her kitchen with an inconsolable baby.

Christina drops her purse and shrugs off her coat, steps

over a cat to get to us. "Wait," she says excitedly. "He likes the Kinks! Alexa, play 'Pictures in the Sand'!" Christina dances around us, singing the lyrics and catching Landon's attention.

"If I didn't have a dime,
Would you still be loving me?
While I spend my whole life through,
Drawing pictures just for you.
But I could never draw my love,
It's so very hard to do.
Pictures in the sand,
Writing messages to you..."

I dance around with Landon in my arms. My grandson loves The Kinks? Naturally! Look where he's sprouting. His tears stop. By the time Cassidy walks into our party, laden with her heavy college backpack, he is beaming. ⬢

THE ELEVATOR
CATHERINE DENUNZIO

A hand shot through, reversing the doors.
Four riders entered—polite nods, thank-yous—
varying in age, size, and color.

But when I murmured *an elevator of women*
just loudly enough to be heard,
faces lifted and brightened, heads
nodded, soft chuckles tumbled about.

Then, the one who'd stopped
the closing doors, spoke:

That's right. That is right!
All . . . women.
Strong. And safe!
Smart. And be-autiful!

Sounds of assent rose with each declaration.
The elevator hummed, at some point stopped.
We nodded—smiles holding—slipped back
into ourselves, and stepped out into the lobby.

But as I drove home, I reviewed her words.

Strong I got—because we must be.
And safe—when those doors closed, no one
had to go to the familiar wondering.
Smart? I was not sure—but maybe smart.
Smart to assume the strength, to understand the safety.

And beautiful?
As a stand of cedars.
A field of moss-covered boulders.
A tidal marsh fringed by grasses.

Beautiful?
You should have seen us. ⬧

REQUIEM FOR A FIREFLY
KARA MOLWAY RUSSELL

"The charismatic firefly faces extinction."
Late-arriving guest of dusky backyard barbecues,
she turned heads, then—
darting in and out the arborvitae hedgerow
(thinning in places, but still more hedge than gap) and now
she's back to grabbing headlines

Clickbait.
"Her flashing abdomen attracts and signals suitors."
Not suitors, always, but fat-fisted children
jamming leaves into jelly jars "for food"

I remember the weight of my own dimpled jar,
The tick-kick of fluttering wings on glass.
I knew (and she knew) the meaning of *endangered* then.

Who will believe this winged-dinosaur emitted her
own light?
Who will believe she once took flight?

(The author does not specify some species do not fly.)

"Light pollution" is all he says:
sex signals out of sync.

I stop to mourn the passing of the charismatic
soft-bodied beetle of summer,
victim of ambient light—

click shut the page
and lie beside my husband in the pitch black,

flightless. 🛡

MOON ON A HALF SHELL
JOANIE DIMARTINO

"At 4 a.m. the Cook jumped overboard having lain
in the *Moon* all night he was out of his head."
—Charles W. Morgan, logbook, July 8, 1846

Drowsy orb, the hue
of dried sea salts,

froths forth the opaque tides
we sail upon, each season passes

unheeded on the sea:
our years brim with tooth

and bone polished
to a sheen like flecks

of reflected light
set in iridescent nebulae,

or a gloss of whale oil gleamed
over crested currents

when morning looms—
a sextant useless, I study

this emerald celestial swirl
hissing in the Arctic

firmament, a luminous
crackling glint above— alone

on deck, I stand under a sky
shucked open

into plums, indigos, mottled tar
dark, yet white capped

and milk spilled: distant, spherical,
storytelling—

among constellations I seek
a whale's eye, a blowhole,

starry water droplets
from a fancied surfaced fluke,

abalone imaginings in my aubade,
this aurora, where the moon's

a pearl, a stone,
some slick oyster, maybe. ◈

ANGELS AND DEMONS
AMY SISSON

"Once upon a time, there were three very different little girls...who grew up to be three very different women. But they have three things in common: They're brilliant, they're beautiful, and they work for me. My name is Charlie."
— *Charlie's Angels* the movie, 2000

1.

On the brimming cusp of puberty, me and my sisters, Katie and Liz, would oftentimes be rock stars in the latest, flashiest MTV music videos. We were doctors, nurses, and patients. We were teachers or students playing school. We were guests on our very own *The Jerry Springer Show*, taping live from the living room!" We were priests pretending to give the holy sacrament of flattened white bread cut to resemble communion; Holy Hawaiian Punch, our blood of Christ. Out back in the small area of woods behind our house in a small Connecticut town, we disappeared into our make-believe world. The scattered maze of crisscrossed fallen trees created the perfect stage for some of our most dramatic scenes. We once dug to China. That was messy.

One day my aunt and uncle interrupted us playing *Charlie's Angels*. We imitated the super-detective ladies—we karate chopped the air while flipping face forward into small piles of slowly accumulating snow. My sisters and I used our imaginations to escape the chaos brewing under the roof of our home. Our laughs seemed not to overpower the yelling and screaming that progressively grew louder from our small, blue house. That day would be one of our parents' last major fights. My memory is choppy, but I remember being confused to see my aunt and uncle. The cops were there too, but they got called frequently enough for us not to be overly alarmed.

My mom cried hysterically as my dad yelled in her face; police officers acted as referees between the two. Our neighbors sheepishly returned to their peaceful home across the street. My sisters and I were quickly ushered to the car with no time to even grab an overnight bag. As we pulled away in the backseat of my aunt's car, I read the profanities spray-painted across my mom's car and onto the walls of the garage. The faded marks remain red to this day. The silent ride allowed for the echoes of the day to haunt us the entirety of the drive. That was a messy day.

2.

As children, we learned how to conceal evidence. For over a decade, a calendar hung on the closet door in the hallway to hide a hole. Maybe it was caused from a household item being thrown—the coffee pot or vacuum. Maybe a fist? I don't recall what specific event that led to the hole in the door, but we covered it. The fragmented wood indented perfectly in the middle. The calendar served as a way of hiding our family's anger: the slow dismantling of our family unit. We kept it hidden away from the outside world. But within our small house on Hughes Street, it would seep into every available crevice, including our psyches.

The chaos was normal though. Fights typically ended with my dad packing up and leaving for a couple days—not that I have a lot of memories of him being present. It was believed he traveled a lot for work, but his particular whereabouts were always questionable. I do remember when he was there, it was destructive. Toxic. Loud. Erratic. I have a vague recollection of the day he lifted our bulky, all metal vacuum cleaner and threw it across the living room to where my mom and oldest sister Katie sat in the gray, living room recliner. I'd oftentimes sit behind that chair and hide—a small, safe sanctuary. Katie recently asked me if I remembered this incident. I explained to her, I could only recall what she has talked about before.

She said, "I was petrified and I remember Mom sitting stoically in front of me." We talked about how any of our "good" memories with dad are recalled by family photos, like fishing trips or family celebrations. I told her of the only memory I have of laying on the couch with him. But I can't seem to decipher whether it's an actual memory, or if my mind has somehow convinced itself that it's from that one picture I've seen of us together.

3.

Our classic family trip to Disney was anything but a happy memory. My sisters and I were all under the age of eight and the only thing we all collectively recall from that vacation was my parents incessant arguing. It started with the rental car.

"Whose brilliant idea was it to rent a convertible with three little girls and several bags of luggage?" my mother had grumbled from the passenger seat. Or when the keys to the hotel room were misplaced and caused an uproar of anger followed by awkward and strained hours of the silent treatment. It seemed the families that surrounded us had some secret recipe to remaining happy, playful, and connected. My mom would spend ten years of her life paying off the credit card my dad used to pay for that trip. He was determined to "give us the best experience of our lives." He had to bring his girls to Disney—fulfilling society's ideal of what the "all-American, happy family" does—the exact opposite of what we actually were. I would have traded in that whole vacation to have had the five of us connect lovingly. That was a messy vacation.

4.

Around the age of seven, I remember chasing my Mom's car halfway down the street. I ran desperately after her, convinced she was leaving for good. It typically wasn't my mom that left after big blowouts with my dad. I cried hysterically for hours curled up in a ball under the covers of my bed. My imagination running wild as to what our lives would be like being stuck there with just dad. Who would he project his rage on now? Would he get just as angry at us, for…God knows what? The underlying anxieties accumulated, layering themselves on top of the emotional rubbish from the last episode. It's similar to the way one snowflake turns into a light layering, which in turn accumulates inch by inch until you're waist deep. One erratic episode turns into another resentment, into yet another unresolved issue. A child growing up in such an atmosphere flips face forward into the snowbank, and does what? Is she then, in that moment, faced with the reality of the depths of psychological damage from growing up in such an atmosphere? Of course not. That happens years later, after the solace of a wooded area out back no longer protects her and her two sisters.

5.

I have a single memory of holding my dad's hand that didn't come from a captured moment behind a lens. It was the time my grandmother begged, then bribed, my sister Liz and me to go visit my dad in prison. It was a couple years after my parents' divorce was finalized when I was around thirteen or fourteen. I recall everything about the experience being cold. The metal seat I sat on, cold. The air of the open building, cold. The tall ceilings and metal beams above, cold. The plastic covers of the fluorescent lights were filthy, giving off a dull light to an already depressing room. The smell of the room was pungent with despair. My leg, covered by my skinny jeans, felt cold against the metal leg that went down the center of the round table. My dad sat across from the three of us. My grandmother planted directly between my sister and me. My dad reached out his cold, sweaty hand and loosely held my fingers. We didn't know the specifics of the charges against him, but we had enough information to assume it had something to do with a domestic dispute with his girlfriend at the time. His pale, chunky fingers seemed swollen. Perhaps I had never looked at my father's hands so closely, but they were ghostly transparent. I let no more than a couple seconds pass before I pulled back my hand and tucked it quickly between my thighs. Even my demeanor of that day was cold. A chill that takes a lifetime to shake.

6.

Katie and I often take smoke rides along a reservoir in our hometown. We roll a joint as a way of connecting. The other day we were driving and we started comparing our "crazies." She lit the piece with three clicks of her red lighter, inhaling deeply.

"I literally overthink everything he says," she said as she passed me the joint. I reached for it without looking away from the road. I twisted it a few times between my thumb and index finger, then lifted it to my lips to inhale. I held it there for a minute, then exhaled and coughed. "Me too. I create the most ridiculous stories in my head about what he 'probably' means or 'meant' to say." I took another hit. She nodded and said, "I make myself so anxiety ridden, I don't even know how to calm myself down." I passed it back to her and looked at her briefly. "Why do you think my phone is shattered? I threw it down the stairs the other night because I got so mad at him for not coming to see me because 'I felt alone.'" She took a longer puff. We continued looking aimlessly at the winding road ahead. I watched her turn her head towards the pitch-black water.

7.

There's a small picture in a teal frame I keep in a junk drawer. My sister Liz had it buried in the bottom of a box she once brought back home from college. The snapshot captures a moment of time so entirely at odds with the memories of my father. It is of me, my father, and Liz doing facial masks together. It was taken at his girlfriend's house—the one he had cheated on my mom with after eighteen years of marriage. The same woman who sent him to prison. I remember liking her because there were virtually no rules or supervision when we went to stay with them. I felt so guilty for my fondness towards the woman who had caused my mom to spend so many nights crying in the bathroom.

This was the postdivorce/preincarceration period of time. We look so happy in the photo. You wouldn't know from the picture the depths of our desire for healthy love from this man. My dad is shirtless, looking somewhat disoriented. Now I know he was heavily medicated on prescription drugs. The beginning stages of an addiction to legal narcotics, among all the other substance abuse problems my dad has had throughout his lifetime. My sister Liz sat directly next to him in her silk pajamas with little pink and red hearts. I leaned into my sister from the far right wearing my favorite purple-striped tank top. I saved money for months in order to afford that shirt from Limited Too. All three of us have pieces of the translucent mask peeling from our faces. I sometimes wonder why Liz had thrown this picture into a box of junk. Is it because the look of our excitement being with dad broke her heart? I can relate. The photo used to lay flat next to the drawer, but it hurt too much to look at. I make sure to keep it buried underneath hair clips and bobby pins and lipsticks and rings. I can't seem to throw it out either. I guess we all heal in our own time.

8.

After spending many months in therapy, many years separated from my childhood, I started to recognize that it wasn't my fault I had become so emotionally cold towards the world. My insecurities and lack of emotional control did not arise out of nowhere. I know the exact session it all started to click. I sat frustrated on my therapist's plush, purple couch, the type of furniture you would expect to see in a Victorian-style home. I felt especially alone and unloved in this moment, as if not a single person on this earth could fulfill this deep-rooted hole in my heart. I spoke slowly, letting the hiccups of hysterics work their way out in between words. "I think the only way my sisters and I learned how to survive our childhood was by escaping and pretending to be elsewhere...." She sat quietly in her chair a few feet across from me, nodding slowly. We didn't say much after that. The safety of her small office, with slanted ceilings and subdued lighting, reminded me of the days I would hide as a child. I wiped my tears with an already too-used tissue. She sat just as silently, making sure to meet my eyes every time they looked toward hers. We had been working towards this realization for months.

9.

About a year after my epiphany in therapy, Katie and I sat in our large rental jeep during one of the final evenings on our trip to Hawaii. My sister Liz had planned, paid for, and created daily itineraries for our family trip to Oahu. She had surprised my mom with the invitation for Mother's Day and extended that to Katie, Liz's girlfriend, Claire, and myself for a nine day trip. It had been a dream of my mom's to see Hawaii, and here we were. The cotton candy skies gave hint of the early evening. We headed out on the open road away from our rental house towards the more populated areas of Upper Island. Five minutes down the road, our heads turned toward each other with a nod, and she pulled the vehicle over. We exited, climbed onto the sides, and popped off the two-piece top. I couldn't help but think, *Let's air out this stifling tension that has been slowly building these last couple days. The cool evening air would help clear it out.* She pulled the vehicle back on the road and we continued. We didn't need to speak. Our silence said enough. We didn't know where we were headed, but we wanted to be out.

Moments later, we started to hear and feel the patter of light rain. We quickly pulled back onto the side of the road and scrambled to get the top back on. We laughed uncontrollably as the pouring rains drenched our bodies from the sweet Hawaiian skies. The two-lane roadway allowed for my seat on the passenger side to be the perfect outlook. I looked longingly at the endless fields of tall grass that stretched until they met the bottom of the mountains. In that moment, I wanted to go back and hold that sobbing little girl curled up in her childhood bed and whisper in her ear that it would all be ok. I pictured the three of us propelling ourselves to the top of Mount Ka'ala's peak to release an exhaustive scream at the top of our lungs, and then allowing the water to wash away the weight of all our sorrows.

10.

The other day, I rolled over and stood up as a twenty-eight-year-old with the strength of a Charlie's Angel. I had gotten myself out of an abusive, oftentimes violent, and completely unstable relationship I had somehow found myself in. (The cycle of domestic abuse had crept its way out of my memory and into my life. The reminder of that scared young child, hysterically crying in her bed reappeared so many years later.) How do you even begin to unbury and heal the pain evoked from such experiences? I suppose we let our spirits break just a little bit, and we use our powerful imaginations to raise us to the top of mountains and scream until it feels just a little better. Or we schedule our therapy appointments. And even when it is the absolute hardest thing we do, we show up, and we continue to heal. ♥

EPIPHANY
JASON COURTMANCHE

A solstice moon, almost full.
Waning gibbous.
Some stars. Not many.
City lights, streetlights,
illuminate the sky, the pavement.
An empty space near the emergency room entrance.
Blue lights. Red lights.
Soft noises of blunted crisis.
Mute sadness seeps through the sliding doors
and granulates in the cold night air,
becomes something solid and small
that can be breathed into the lungs and metastasize
like coal dust, like asbestos, like fear.
Yellow lines on the pavement are faded
and lead away toward a not-so-distant interstate,
on ramps and off ramps, the hum of traffic.
A parking garage.
An abandoned department store.

A skywalk leading to an empty building.
In the other direction, a neighborhood
of once majestic Victorians.
Boards on windows.
Metal stairwells to second-floor apartments.
Bars on first-floor windows.
Empty lots.
An old car, tireless,
its axle rods resting on dirt
and cinder blocks,
clumps of grass persisting against the odds
for no other reason than that they must. ◈

LINES COMPOSED MANY MILES FROM TUCSON
EMI GONZALEZ

Just beyond the quarry wall
resembling Stonehenge
a molten lava sky is effortlessly
showcased
before you
like burning embers
the remains of a lofty fire
a séance for the end of a decade
you tell me
that you never understood God's artistry
until you witnessed your first Catalina sky
combustible claret-infused mountains
Seeping sanguine
smoldering strokes
This awe-inspiring backdrop
another nightly masterpiece
or an example of

the Romantics' notion of sublimity
here, across the street from the Connecticut River
I sit at my white bistro patio set
subtly rusting
and imagine you, so small and insignificant
stained with sun's dusky afterglow
Quietly sitting at yours 🛡️

FOR THE LOVE OF LINEN
NANCY MCMILLAN

I pull my lilac linen shirt out of the washer and shake it to ease out the wrinkles. Then, I drape it over my arm while I load the rest of the damp clothes into the dryer. I shut the door, set the dryer to permanent press, then head upstairs, linen shirt in hand, to the sound of the dryer falling into its soothing rhythm. In the bathroom, I hang the shirt on a thick plastic hanger, positioning it so the shoulder seams line up with the hanger. I smooth the collar, pressing the pointed tabs, then button it all the way down, smoothing it out with my palms, and do the same with the sleeves, pressing them into a wrinkle-free shape. The damp fabric feels cool and pleasant under my hands. I stand in the bathroom, illuminated by the hall light, and adjust the shirt on the hanger with one final smoothing. It looks ready for a store window display. The fabric, made from a natural material, reminds me of summer.

Linen, smooth and cool to the touch, is at home on the beach, in the sun, on an August evening. Perhaps its association with the lightness, freedom, and ease of summer is why I love it. It looks beautiful once ironed, but the effect doesn't last. Once worn, it wrinkles immediately, one flaw you must accept when you wear it. It is always accompanied with nonchalance.

I own a pale-pink linen dress of simple design, with a dropped waist and a V-neck, sleeveless, and most importantly, with the coveted pockets. My mother, gone now twenty years, brought it home from the tony Fairfield County thrift store where she volunteered Friday mornings. Friday was the day donations were sorted, giving her first shot at choosing clothes for me, her daughter who shared her taste. Of course I shared her taste. She trained me to be the clotheshorse I became.

In high school, I kept a desk calendar of what I wore to school. My goal: to not repeat an outfit for three weeks. I achieved this goal with my mother's help, through her sewing skills and her love of shopping. Unsure of myself in so many ways, fashion gave me a place I could present a mask of confidence. It was my idea to track my clothes, but it was her pleasure I was courting with the attention to my daily outfit, a bond I desired to strengthen.

Historically, a clotheshorse was a wooden frame to hang clothes to dry, something I could use today. In the 1800s, the term came to describe both men and women who were passionate about fashion and always dressed in the latest styles. A fashion plate. I was the first girl in my high school to wear a tailored, pearl-gray midi coat with a miniskirt underneath, quite the statement in the early seventies. I also wore custom-made dresses, stitched from Liberty London fabric. My mother displayed her sewing skill by the way she cut the fabric, precisely positioning the blue, italicized logo to run along the back zipper. I dropped my clotheshorse identity in college, but still chose purple suede clogs and caftans as part of my wardrobe. Now, as an adult with a disposable income, I fell in love with linen.

One of the oldest textiles on the planet, linen's origin dates back to 3500 BC Egypt, where linen was used for shrouds and symbolized light, purity, and wealth. The fabric is made from the interior stem of the flax plant, exposed after retting, or soaking. It is then dried, crushed, and beaten to prepare it to be spun. None of the plant is wasted: the seeds are used to produce linseed oil, flaxseed, soaps, paper, and cattle feed. A member of the Linaceae family, the second part of its Latin name, *Linum usitatissimum*, means "most useful." The simple, five-petal flowers grow and glow in shades of blue ranging from pale blue to periwinkle.

I still own that pale-pink linen dress, the one with pockets my mother gave me. It's my beach dress. I wear it over a wet swimsuit, sometimes with that lilac linen shirt. Layers of linen seem ridiculous in their luxury, yet the fabric is derived from a humble plant grown in fields halfway around the world. I have mended this dress, patching the threadbare spots, and still more frayed spots appear. Yet, I don't give it up. I will continue to mend it until it falls apart. When it does, I will place it in the drawer with the other objects I can't give up because they, too, are imbued with meaning.

Layers of my identity are woven into this piece of clothing: daughter, lover of domestic pleasures, mender of objects. Every time I pull the dress from my closet, I remember when my mother handed it to me, ironed and on a hanger. I recall how she ran her fingertips across the fabric, the smile we shared, and how her blue eyes lit up when she said, "and it has pockets."

I remain my mother's daughter. ◑

CONTRIBUTORS

Janet L. Bannister is a lifelong Connecticut resident currently planted in Coventry, Connecticut. An empty nester, direct-care worker, and recent graduate of Eastern Connecticut State University, Bannister spends most of her time reading, writing, hiking the blue-blazed trails of CT, kayaking local ponds and lakes, honing home-renovation skills, and haunting libraries and pubs. She writes fiction, creative nonfiction, and poetry, with her work often centering on themes of nature, spirituality, psychology, and loss.

Charles V. Belson is a Connecticut architect, photographer, and writer. His published nonfiction essays include *Reinterpreting Palladio's Villa Rotonda*, and *For some of us, jury duty doesn't really end at the courthouse*. His work has appeared in *Period Homes Magazine*, *The New York Times*, and publications produced by the Harvard University–Boston Museum of Fine Arts Expedition in Egypt. He lives in Norwalk with his wife Janer. She's the focal point of his story *Rendezvous*.

Playwright Susan Cinoman is a frequent contributor on ABC's *The Goldbergs*. Her plays have been seen Off-Broadway and at Ensemble Studio Theatre, Naked Angels, and Circle Repertory Company. Her awards include Guilford Performing Arts Prize in Drama, Capital Repertory Theatre's Next Act! Festival, Gulfshore Playhouse Selection, the Best Connecticut Filmmaker Award in 2009, the Best Narrative Film at New England Film and Video Festival; an Official Selection by the International Berkshire Film Festival, and the Maxwell Anderson Playwright Prize.

Ginny Lowe Connors is the author of several poetry collections, including *Toward the Hanging Tree: Poems of Salem Village*. Her chapbook, *Under the Porch*, won the Sunken Garden Chapbook Poetry Prize, and she has earned numerous awards for individual poems. As publisher of her own press, Grayson Books, Connors has also edited numerous poetry anthologies, including *Forgotten Women: A Tribute in Poetry*. She is coeditor of *Connecticut River Review*.

Jason Courtmanche is Assistant Professor in residence in English, an affiliate faculty in teacher education, director of the Connecticut Writing Project, and an assistant coordinator of the UConn Early College Experience in English. Recent academic publications have appeared in *Profession, Writing Program Administration, Deep Reading, Nathaniel Hawthorne Review, Resources for American Literary Study, Writers Who Teach, What Does it Mean to be White in America?, What Is "College-Level" Writing?, Vol. 2*, and *Nathaniel Hawthorne in the College Classroom*.

Catherine DeNunzio has published poetry in *Many Mountains Moving; The Breath of Parted Lips: Voices from The Robert Frost Place, Vol. II*; and *Teacher-Writer 2015, Vol. VII*. She has work upcoming in *Italian Americana*. She is a member of the Westerly, Rhode Island Savoy Poetry Salon. A graduate of the University of Connecticut (BA, MA), DeNunzio lives in Connecticut with her husband and their ridiculous dog.

Joanie DiMartino has work published in many literary journals and anthologies, including *Modern Haiku, Alimentum, Calyx,* and *Circe's Lament: An Anthology of Wild Women*. She is a past winner of the Betty Gabehart Award for Poetry. DiMartino is the author of two collections of poetry, *Licking the Spoon* and *Strange Girls*, and is completing her third manuscript about the 19th-century whaling industry, for which she was a 38th Voyager on the *Charles W. Morgan*.

Meghan Evans earned her master's degree in creative writing from Sarah Lawrence College. She teaches literature and writing at Central Connecticut State University and, until recently, taught creative writing at the Academy of Arts.

Maura Faulise is an Assistant Professor of Writing and Literature at the Community College of Rhode Island. She completed her Master of Arts in Teaching at Brown University and currently studies poetry and fiction through Pacific University's Master of Fine Arts in Writing program. She resides with her family in rural Connecticut.

A recent graduate of Central Connecticut State University, Kathryn Fitzpatrick is pursuing an MFA at the University of Alabama. Her work appears in *Out Magazine, Cleaver Magazine, Bodega Magazine, Gravel,* and elsewhere. She recently coedited *Flash Nonfiction Food* (Woodhall Press, 2020) alongside Tom Hazuka, and she is writing a collection of essays about her Connecticut hometown, Thomaston, called *Raggie.*

After years of working for media, higher education, and nonprofit organizations, Beth Gibbs is "free-tired" and pursuing her passions of writing, teaching yoga, and leading workshops on personal growth and healthy aging. She uses her energy and sense of humor to inspire, inform, and entertain. She is the author of *Ogi Bogi, The Elephant Yogi.* Her next book, *Enlighten Up! The Five Layers of Self-Awareness,* will be released in October. She blogs at bethgibbs.com.

Cecilia Gigliotti is a writer, musician, photographer, and general documentarian who holds the MA in English Literature from Central Connecticut State University. Her poem "Igor Stravinsky Awaits the Arrival of Dylan Thomas" won Blue Muse magazine's Leslie Leeds Poetry Prize in 2018; other works have appeared in publications including *The Atticus Review, Plainsongs, Boudin, Outrageous Fortune, The Route 7 Review, Riza, Uncomfortable Revolution*, and *DoveTales: Writing for Peace*. A native of New Britain, Connecticut, she now lives in Berlin, Germany.

Nichole Gleisner teaches French language and literature at Southern Connecticut State University. A writer and translator, she also serves as poetry editor at *the New Haven Review* and has lived in Connecticut for the last nine years.

Sitara Gnanaguru is an Indian-American writer and lifelong Nutmegger. She is a proud alumna of the University of Connecticut, where she studied English. When she's not reading or writing poetry, you can find her outdoors exploring new parks and trails or frequenting her favorite coffee shops.

Emi Gonzalez grew up in Connecticut and has been writing poetry since she was a child. Her poetry has been published in several anthologies, including *Caduceus*, the journal of Yale Medical Group and Art Place. She is a member of the Guilford Shoreline Poets and is a PhD student at the University of Tennessee, Knoxville in Literature, Criticism, and Textual Studies. There she works on the editorial team for *Grist*, UT's nationally distributed literary journal.

José B. González is the author of *Toys Made of Rock* and *When Love Was Reels*. His poetry has been anthologized in the *Norton Introduction to Literature* and *The Wandering Song: Central American Writing in the United States* and has appeared in journals including *Callaloo, Palabra,* and *Acentos Review*. A Fulbright Scholar, he is the co-editor of *Latino Boom: An Anthology of U.S. Latino Literature* and editor of latinostories.com.

Benjamin S. Grossberg's books include *Space Traveler* (University of Tampa, 2014) and *Sweet Core Orchard* (University of Tampa, 2009), winner of the Tampa Review Prize and a Lambda Literary Award. His poems have appeared widely in the *Pushcart Prize* and the *Best American Poetry* anthologies, and the magazines *Paris Review, Kenyon Review, The Southern Review,* and *The Sun*. His new collection, *My Husband Would*, will be published by the University of Tampa Press this fall.

Dr. Avery Jenkins is a former award-winning journalist and essayist who took a twenty-five-year break from the writing world to become a chiropractor and acupuncturist. He holds a second-degree black belt in the martial art of aikido and is in his final year of training to become a Daoist priest. Dr. Jenkins lives in northwest Connecticut with his wife and two dogs of uncertain temperament.

Recently named the inaugural poet laureate of Ridgefield, Connecticut, B. Fulton Jennes engages the community in writing, reading, and discussing poetry. Her poems have appeared/will appear in *Tupelo Quarterly 20, Connecticut River Journal, Frost Meadow Review,* the *Connecticut Poetry Anthology 2020,* and other publications. Jennes also serves as the poet-in-residence for the Aldrich Contemporary Art Museum where she develops poetry programming and events. She advises the Shifting Static Poets, a teen slam-poetry team.

Sarah Darer Littman is the critically-acclaimed author of young adult novels including *Deepfake*, *Backlash* (winner of the Iowa Teen Award and Grand Canyon Reader Award) and *Want to Go Private?*. She also writes humorous, middle-grade novels: *Taming of the Shoe*, *Fairest of Them All*, *Charmed, I'm Sure*, and *Confessions of a Closet Catholic*. Littman teaches in the MFA program at Western Connecticut State University and at the Yale Writers' Workshop. Visit her online at sarahdarerlittman.com.

Kiran Masroor is a sophomore at Yale University where she's studying neuroscience under the pre-med track. On campus, she's involved with the TEETH Slam Poetry group, as well as Yalies for Pakistan. She loves playing the piano, working with children, and reading Joy Harjo's works.

A resident of Hartford, Melissa McEwen says Hartford is her muse when writing poetry. Her poem "Slice of Life Sestina," about a group of Hartford boys, was published in *Connecticut River Review* and nominated for the Pushcart Prize. Her work has also been published in multiple publications such as *Rattle*, *Blue Fifth Review*, and *Role Call: A Generational Anthology of Social & Political Black Literature & Art*, to name a few.

Claudia McGhee has dealt in and with words for decades as a software-technical writer, newspaper columnist, freelance editor, eBook producer, poet, essayist, and fiction writer. McGhee's chapbook of poems, *Paperlight*, was published by Finishing Line Press. Her technical writing has been translated into six languages and distributed across Europe, South America, and Japan, and now that she is retired, she is working to ensure her poems, memoir, and science fiction read properly in American English.

Nancy McMillan of Bethlehem is the award-winning author of *March Farm: Season by Season on a Connecticut Family Farm*. Her essays and articles have appeared in Connecticut newspapers and magazines. In her writing classes at Arts Escape Inc. in Southbury, she helps students embrace and inhabit their innate creativity. She is currently at work on a novel. Find more at nancymcmillan.com where she blogs about pies, writing, music, and connection.

Jean P. Moore is a novelist, poet, and nonfiction writer. Her award-winning novel, *Tilda's Promise*, was published in September of 2018. Her work has appeared in newspapers, magazines, and literary journals, such as the *Harford Courant, The Philadelphia Inquirer, UpStreet,* and the *SNReview*. Her novel, *Water on the Moon*, published in 2014, won the 2015 Independent Publisher Book Award for contemporary fiction. Her chapbook, *Time's Tyranny*, was published by Finishing Line Press in 2017.

Steven Ostrowski is a fiction writer, poet, painter, and teacher. His work appears widely in literary journals, magazines, and anthologies. He is the author of five published chapbooks—four of poems and one of stories. He and his son, Ben, are authors of a full-length collaboration called *Penultimate Human Constellation*, published in 2018 by Tolsun Books. His chapbook, *After the Tate Modern*, won the 2017 Atlantic Road Prize and was published in 2018 by Island Verse Editions. His short story, "Even on Good Nights," was a finalist for American Short Fiction's Short(er) Fiction Award and will be published in the fall of 2020. He teaches at Central Connecticut State University.

Makenzie Ozycz is a graduate student at Central Connecticut State University, pursuing a master's degree in English literature. Her previously published works include two nonfiction CCSU sponsored magazines, *Terra Infirma* and *The Reentry Magazine*, as well as a short nonfiction blog published on CCSU's literary magazine, *Blue Muse*. Ozycz was also nominated for the Leslie Leeds Poetry Prize in 2020. She hopes to continue her writing career post-graduation.

Aimee Pozorski is professor of English at Central Connecticut State University where she directs the English MA Program and codirects the minor in American studies. She is co-executive editor of *Philip Roth Studies*, a peer-reviewed journal published by Purdue University Press.

Kara Molway Russell teaches Shakespeare at Central Connecticut State University. She holds a PhD in Renaissance Literature from the University of Rochester where it snowed steadily for four and a half of the five years she was enrolled there. She is mom to two teenage boys, one of whom recently urged her to get busy doing what she truly loves, and she's been writing ever since. This is her first poem. Follow her blog at innuendoandirony.com.

Connecticut State University distinguished professor, Vivian Shipley, has taught at Southern Connecticut State University full time since 1969. She was awarded a 2020-21 Connecticut Office of the Arts Artist Fellowship for Poetry. Nominated for the Pulitzer Prize, her twelfth book, *An Archaeology of Days*, was published by Negative Capability Press in 2019 and was named the 2020-21 Paterson Poetry Prize Finalist. *All of Your Messages Have Been Erased*, (2010, SLU) won the 2011 Paterson Award for Sustained Literary Achievement, among other accolades.

Amy Sisson currently works as a literacy tutor. She's always had a passion for writing, but never allotted for the focus and seriousness to the craft. After four years of absence from pursuing her bachelor's in English, she went back to finish her three remaining classes. One of which was a creative writing course where her excitement towards writing was reignited. She is excited for her future as an English teacher and part-time writer!

Katherine Szpekman writes poetry and memoir from her home in Collinsville, Connecticut. Her work has appeared in *Red Eft Review, Sky Island Journal, Muddy River Poetry Review, Chestnut Review, Sheila-Na-Gig, Hiram Poetry Review*, and *Three Line Poetry*. She was awarded Honorable Mention in the Connecticut River Review Poetry Contest 2019.

Wendy Tarry was born and raised in Ottawa, Canada but now makes her home on the Connecticut Shoreline. Tarry holds degrees in English and Education from the University of Ottawa and a Master's in Divinity from Queen's University. The author of "With a Whisper: The Poetry of Wendy Tarry", she enjoys working in a local library, assisting with worship at her church and exploring Connecticut with her husband and their two daughters.

Mika Taylor got her MFA at the University of Arizona. She's been supported by numerous grants and residency awards including the University of Wisconsin, the Ucross Foundation, the Atlantic Center for the Arts, the Sewanee Writers Conference, and the Wesleyan Writers Conference. She received a 2019 Artistic Excellence Grant from the State of Connecticut. Her stories and essays have appeared in *Granta, Tin House, Ninth Letter*, the *Kenyon Review, Guernica*, and others. Read more at mikataylor.com.

Marina Tinone is a writer based in Connecticut. Their work primarily focuses on language, identity, and voice. They create the things they wish they could have held when they were growing up. You can visit them online at mtinone.com.

Jason Wilkins is a writer currently sequestered in Connecticut.